The Guide to
Good Corporate Citizenship

Marie Jennings

The Guide to
Good Corporate Citizenship

Published in association with the Institute of Directors

DIRECTOR BOOKS

Published by Director Books,
an imprint of Fitzwilliam Publishing Limited,
Simon & Schuster International Group,
Fitzwilliam House, 32 Trumpington Street,
Cambridge CB2 1QY, England.

First published 1990

British Library Cataloguing in Publication Data
Jennings, Marie *1930–*
    The guide to good corporate citizenship.
    1. Companies.   Public relations
    I.   Title
    659.285

    ISBN 1-870555-34-1

Designed by Geoff Green
Typeset by Hands Fotoset, Leicester
Printed in Great Britain by BPCC Wheatons Ltd, Exeter

Contents

Foreword

This book should open the eyes, once and for all, of any remaining sceptics in the business world who continue to assert that ethics and profits are incompatible.

Ethics can be defined as applied morality, concentrating on what to do and how to do it rather than on the whys and whethers. Tackled from this standpoint, the close convergence between the behaviour required to run an ethical business and a profitable business – a 'good' business in both senses – becomes very clear. Three aspects are especially important:

- No business can be good by accident; objectives must be defined, policies and strategies devised, responsibilities assigned and performance monitored.

- No business can be good unless it pays the most scrupulous attention to the needs and aspirations of all the people associated with it or affected by it.

- No business can be good unless it is properly led by its board.

These propositions form the basis of most successful approaches to business management, and they stand out equally clearly in the following pages devoted to good corporate citizenship.

Anyone, and particularly any director, will find information and ideas here which should prompt careful consideration not only of the many moral issues which people in business face but also of many matters with a clear and direct importance to a company's commercial future.

I hope that as many directors as possible will read what follows and profit from it.

PETER MORGAN
DIRECTOR GENERAL
INSTITUTE OF DIRECTORS

Acknowledgements

I would like to thank, first of all, the experts who went out of their way to help me with the development of this book, in particular Sir John Harvey-Jones and David Bernstein, two distinguished communicators; Doug Ann Newsom, of the Department of Journalism, Texas Christian University; and Meredith Fernstrom, Vice President in charge of Public Responsibility at American Express, New York.

I should like, too, to thank all the contributors to Part II of the book: Dr Elizabeth Nelson, Adam Dupre, Colin Adamson, the late Edgar Palamountain, Tom Dodd, Janet Brady, Caroline Kay and Brian Locke. Their specialist knowledge of their areas has brought much of value for the reader to absorb.

To Professor Jack Mahoney, of King's College Business Ethics Research Centre, University of London, and to Michael Webber, Chairman and Managing Director of Pifco Limited, my grateful thanks for the time they spent giving me guidance and reading through the text of the book for comment before publication.

Grateful thanks, too, to Sue Williams in Gloucestershire for helping with the administration of the entire exercise and for gathering all the threads together, checking and ensuring that the text included all the updating information necessary. Also to my husband, Brian Locke for providing a ready ear for discussion of the issues involved and for his meticulous help in checking the manuscript.

Listen, decide, persuade – that has been the key to good communications over the years. I thank all those who helped me to listen, and to decide what should go into this book. I hope that they will feel that the result goes some way towards the important job of persuading business that good corporate citizenship is an important and vital aid to good business in the years ahead.

MARIE JENNINGS

Introduction: Why this book?

The reasons why I wanted to write this book are simple to understand. They are also fundamental. The first is that, with advances in communications, transport and information technology, more people can become more aware of each other, and more rapidly, than ever before. The actions we take constantly impinge on others. The decisions we make affect many people other than ourselves. It is important, therefore, to identify the important decisions taken in business and to know their extent and implications. It is important, also, to be able to judge and identify the freedoms we can still enjoy, now, and those we hope to be able to enjoy in the future.

The responsibilities of the company director today are far-reaching. They include product and service efficiency as well as the safety of future generations. The second reason for this book is that, in business, we are trained to act responsibly, to act within disciplines and to plan, co-ordinate and implement so as to secure the future success of the individual enterprise, the people who work within it, and the customers, clients and communities it serves. It is important, also, to be mindful of the responsibilities of the business to all these groups, and to shareholders, partners and others (perhaps even the bank manager) who have shown confidence in the enterprise, providing it with investment and other tangible forms of backing.

All this adds up to the company as a corporate citizen. It underlines the importance of reviewing the performance of the company in this area and ensuring the director's practical input. Through business we reach out into the community and the results and effects of each enterprise are judged in the round and relate to the whole, evolving personality of that particular business.

There are four sections in the book. The first focuses on the overall subject area of good corporate citizenship. This automatically takes in the twin areas of corporate responsibility and business ethics. The second includes contributions from distinguished experts on good corporate citizenship in specific areas of activity, for example, marketing, employee relations, customer relations and shareholder relations. This section also covers the company's role with regard to education, the community, charitable giving and sponsorship as well as in its technological and other environments. The third section is devoted to helping the reader understand how to manage the corporate communications function, to get the message across and to ensure that the company makes the most of its case. Finally, the concluding section suggests some important impending changes that will affect the way ahead for business.

It is my submission – and the point I shall be making throughout the pages of this book – that any company, be it a small or medium-size business, or even a large transnational enterprise, has a need to judge whether it is performing as a 'good corporate citizen', and to know the ways and means it can use to improve that performance. It is my belief that knowing and understanding more about this overall area and giving it the high priority it warrants in the overall planning of the business contributes positively to good, profitable business.

Being a good corporate citizen is fundamentally important in relation to overall national prosperity and to the well-being of human beings. This is the first book to bring all these widely different matters and issues together. I hope that readers will find it a useful beginning to what will surely be a developing subject.

PART I

Good corporate citizenship – what it is and why it matters

CHAPTER 1

The starting point

Having acquired this book, the first questions in the mind of the reader will probably be:

- What is good corporate citizenship?
- What does it entail?
- Is it something different, or is it something in which, as a business man or woman, I am already engaged?
- Why should I bother?
- Will any or an increased interest in this area cost me money? If so, how much? And with what conceivable result?

No two individuals or organisations will tackle these questions in the same way, but the reader will find pointers to help find his or her own answers to these and many other questions in the pages of this book.

What is good corporate citizenship?

A citizen is a member of society; so is a company. The role of the company as citizen, locally, nationally and in terms of the global environment within which it operates, will be a key issue for the aspirant business leader of the 1990s. The nature of that role, and the practical ways to maximise it, are the main themes of this book.

Good corporate citizenship consists of being seen to be benevolent to surrounding society, even by an anti-business critic. Its criteria vary with time, so there is no unique set of rules. As well as maintaining industrial, marketing and social progress, an organisation will need to remain solvent, and to stay in being to provide the goods and services that society needs.

To be successful at business and to be thought to conduct good business practice is overwhelmingly the aim of most people in business – given an

3

ideal world. 'Good' business actually equates to good corporate citizenship, as will be seen, but that is not yet realised widely enough.

The world is far from ideal. What, therefore, are the issues which relate to 'good' business and good corporate citizenship? What does 'good corporate citizenship' entail, and is it enough, today, to be one of the many millions of business men and women in the world who believe that they would conduct 'good' business if they could, but that the pressures on them, competitive, economic and personal, make this impossible?

The contention of the author of this book is that the answer to the latter question must be 'no'. Furthermore, that being a good corporate citizen and conducting 'good' ethical business today can benefit the practical bottom line in more ways than one. Indeed, this way could well be the only productive way forward for the company which intends to remain firmly in business, weathering the storms of our changing world.

Sir John Harvey-Jones, one of the best-known and most admired industrialists and a former chairman of ICI, puts the overall issue very finely in a nutshell. He states:

No company exists in a vacuum.

Each of us is dependent upon the goodwill and support of the members of the community in which we exist.

It is only by constantly striving to maintain high ethical and environmental standards that we can renew this 'licence to operate' on which our future depends.

In general terms, the good corporate citizen:

- Offers a consistent and fair deal to its customers over long periods of time.
- Pays more than lip-service to its responsibilities to all its publics – the community in which it operates, its employees (past and present), its shareholders and financial backers, and, of course, its customers – in general it 'serves', in a wide sense, the society of which it is part.
- Is aware of the role it should play in the development of its markets. It is aware, also, of its responsibility to ensure the safety of its products/services, the health of its employees, and of its obligations in the areas of research, education and the environment.
- Identifies itself, above all, as committed to communicating with its different publics accurately, responsibly and effectively, thus ensuring that they are informed on all relevant matters to do with its present and future policies and operations.

In these ways it enhances its reputation and builds confidence and trust in itself. Perhaps more importantly, in these ways it helps to make its market a better place, in the widest senses of those words – efficiently and economically. In so doing, it creates more practical ways in which it can see further ahead and plan its future profitable business.

Good corporate citizenship involves being seen to be benevolent (as well as being so in practice), as well as being effective in a strictly business sense. So standards and criteria of judgement of social and human issues are involved as well as the more technical considerations. And that brings in ethics, too, alongside all the other recognised aspects of industry and commerce. After all, industry and commerce consist of, and involve, people – as workers, as customers, as providers of resources, and even as external regulators, whether politicians or bureaucrats. Those people can work together in the common interest, with urge and initiative and duty of care – which leads to good corporate citizenship based on ethics profitable to all. Or else narrow, short-term, sectional interest can prevail, to the detriment of corporate citizenship and the perversion of ethical standards. Society, which means its individuals both personally and collectively, must choose. A balance must be struck between the extremes of piracy and communism. Commerce and industry have an important role, much of which is not realised by the public. Lessons are continually being learned and applied and they deserve better promulgation. The issues of good corporate citizenship merit ventilation, both internally in companies, and for external understanding via annual reports and general communications. The media can be particularly helpful if mutual trust is established.

There are many environments for a company, especially the biosphere both locally and globally, and the local, personal, social and philosophical environments that are just as important but less easily quantified and observed. The short-sighted company pays little attention to its environment and gets away with what it can burden society with. The good company sees itself as a leading component of society, and develops synergistically with its several environments, responding both to signals and to representations from them. The aim is the responsible and truly efficient use of all resources, to the overall benefit of society. It will be interesting to watch the growth of wider share ownership, and the spread of the worker-shareholder trend and see how corporate citizenship and its ethics evolve.

What is business ethics?

Ethics is the science of morals, rules of conduct, and the basis for conforming to recognised standards. It constitutes the principles by which people can live together successfully in a sustainable society. 'Business ethics' thus provides the principles by which businesses can thrive in a sustainable business and social community. In the words of Professor Jack Mahoney of Kings College, London, the Jesuit director of the Business Ethics Research Centre at the College:

'Of course, the point of business ethics is to prevent good men from going bad'. This comment was made to me in Washington recently by the director of a business ethics centre there.

Today there are certain features of modern business which have brought the subject of business ethics into prominence and they all come down to a vast increase in power and a corresponding increase in public sensitivity. Modern business ethics was born of the rise of corporations and the distinction between ownership and management, coupled with a series of events in the 1960s and 1970s in the US. Those were decades of massive bribery disclosures in the aftermath of Watergate, of the black civil rights and women's movements demanding the eradication of discrimination and stereotyping, of the powerful public safety and environmental lobbies, and of a dawning concern for the plight of the poor and undeveloped peoples of the Third World.

The result was what one commentator termed 'a new social mandate' for business. Human and social values were put firmly on the business agenda, to question the monopoly held by its inhouse values of profitability resulting from rationality and the efficient focusing of resources on financial returns to investors and management.

This book looks at the many different issues involved in that 'new social mandate', giving examples and case histories. But first there is a fundamental question to be asked.

Is good ethics bad for business?

The answer to this question, in a word, is 'no': the opposite should be true, given the practical action necessary to pull the benefits through the company system. Indeed, there are many examples of the sort of horror story which results from not taking the ethical approach. Some appear in Chapter 12 in a technological context, and there are others in various chapters. The cost factors should also be taken into account. The direct costs of not having taken a satisfactory ethical approach today can be large and are clear enough when problems happen in sales, or court cases, or repairing damage. The hidden costs of management time, for example, can also add to the direct costs alarmingly.

In Britain ethics seems to be being taken less seriously than in some other countries. This is potentially a time-bomb capable of damaging the prospects for British business. Given that Japanese children are taught ethics at school and that British children are not, is an important potential commercial advantage being conceded to the world's most effective and aggressive trading nation? Understanding issues and seeing possibilities are attributes worth developing in our future (and present) workers and managers.

Good company ethics is, indeed, an important practical component of sensible overall company management. It is also a realistic basis for doing a job well so that the company and its various types of environment all thrive to their mutual and collective benefit. Whether this is far-seeing benevolence or enlightened self-interest is immaterial: the important thing is to 'do' the business as well as possible for the future as well as for today.

The code of business ethics

Different types of detailed principle or rule can be derived for different types of company in different industries and circumstances. They can include:

- The value to the customer of the goods or services.
- The return to the worker, manager and investor on the effort or resource provided.
- The value to the society and its infrastructure of its 'licence to operate' the business now and in the future.
- The sensible use of raw materials, efficient processing and minimising of waste and pollution.
- Learning from industrial activity and development so that industrial evolution is in harmony with the evolution of the human and natural world.
- Seeing and thinking widely around and ahead of the immediate situation so that what is done provides a reasoned stage for progress into the future.

Accepting these principles and enshrining them in the individual company code of business ethics targeted to the firm's activities will go a long way towards establishing the company as a good corporate citizen. But clearly the most important element in the code is:

- Putting it into practice, and keeping it updated as progress is made both inside the organisation and in society at large.

The practical steps to this end are discussed in the chapters of this book which follow.

The components of good corporate citizenship and business ethics

The components of good corporate citizenship and business ethics should also be inherent in the business plan of the company and in its strategic and development programmes. The mission statement of the company (the agreed principles and targets to which the company works) should clearly identify the role of the organisation as a good corporate citizen; and the company's practices in terms of ethical conduct should stand up to examination. Policy statements prepared by the management team should include relevant sections covering the following areas:

- The company and its markets, customers and suppliers.
- The company and its employees – past, present and future.
- The company and its community.
- The company and its business environment.
- The company and the overall environment.
- The company's role in research and the development of new markets.
- The company's contribution to education.
- The company's sponsorship activities.
- The company and charitable giving.

These areas will form the subject of separate chapters in this book, including relevant case histories.

A new priority?

To the vast majority of businesses good corporate citizenship will not be new. The factor which may be new, however, is that of priority. Today we are living in an age of swiftly changing business and environmental conditions. The priority we should give to the area of good corporate citizenship is high and it is now necessary to pull together all the threads so that a company can answer honestly and fairly when facing the question which is increasingly being posed: 'Is your company acting responsibly?'

The cost of good corporate citizenship to a company

The costs of good corporate citizenship to a company could be minimal – in the main they will be met from existing budgets. Programmes in this area should, indeed, end up contributing to increased profit from increased turnover, especially in the long term. The effort, time and money spent in ways perhaps considered marginal today will return handsome dividends in years to come.

By fusing the interests of the community with those of employees, customers, shareholders and the like, the company should be able to take a much more enlightened and far-sighted view of its responsibilities and of the activities it needs to undertake to meet its commercial objectives.

Here is the view of a distinguished and well-known communicator on good corporate citizenship, David Bernstein, Chairman of The Creative Business Ltd, and a man with a known and respected reputation in the field of effective communications. According to him, the good corporate citizen

- Tells the truth. How else can a company live with itself, let alone with the other citizens who are its neighbours?
- Has a philosophy (or rationale or 'mission statement'). This is a set of corporate beliefs and values which drive the company. It makes sure that every member of the company has a copy.
- Realises that each of its employees is also a citizen – more than that, an ambassador. Each ambassador is fully briefed.
- Sees no reason why all of its publics – clients, suppliers, authorities and its neighbourhood – should not also know its philosophy.
- Tells the community what it stands for: not only will it be better understood, it will have provided criteria by which it asks to be judged. It puts its neck on the block.
- Will err on the side of communicating too much rather than too little. It will aim to be regarded as an open, frank and ready informant. By inviting the attention of the local media, it will probably encourage them to contact it when a story is required.
- Is approachable. It never refuses to talk to the media. It never says 'no comment'. It never fails to keep a promise.
- Holds open house at least once a year. It invites the families of its staff and their friends and its immediate neighbours.
- Is probably far better equipped than any other non-commercial group of people in the locality. Therefore it has amenities (conference rooms, offices, sports facilities) which can be shared and other facilities (copiers, typewriters, slide projectors) which can be made use of.
- Knows that what is appreciated most by the neighbourhood is time – the time of its people on community matters, using their professional expertise, technical skills and commercial experience.
- Does not pollute the neighbourhood. It does as it would be done by. It trusts and earns trust.
- Keeps in touch with local schools, clubs, societies, etc.
- Shows up. It is visible. It does not simply pay money for a quiet life. It is active in the community.
- Initiates projects. It provides ideas, though it does not take them over. It acts as a catalyst and guide.
- Makes sure that the locality gets its fair share of whatever promotional or sponsorship funds it generates. No matter how grand, how multinational, the company never forgets its own part of the local scene.

- Has a community chest at the disposal of a committee. (But community relations is everyone's concern, not solely the committee's.)

Of course all this has benefits for the company; it can be regarded as a form of 'enlightened self-interest'. And there is nothing wrong with that. Nobody will think any the less of the company for it, provided the company is sincere and open – transparency is crucial. Good corporate citizenship is impossible without glasnost.

In conclusion

- Good corporate citizenship to reflect ethical practices is a desirable, practical and potentially profitable commercial objective for a company.
- Achieving a known reputation in this area makes sound, profitable, business sense.
- To achieve results it is important to ensure commitment of intellectual resources at the top level in the company. Only then can planning take place to release the commercially desirable results of initiatives taken.
- In fusing the company interests with those of the community, employees, customers, shareholders and other groups can add to company turnover and company profits.
- The way ahead is not difficult to find – others have found it profitable to travel this path. Hopefully reading this book will enable the reader to draw up a route to follow.

CHAPTER 2

Knowing where the company stands

Having decided that it is worthwhile taking a closer look at the area of corporate citizenship, the first priority will be to judge where the company stands today. It is important to know just how well the company record stands up to close scrutiny. So how does a director set about finding out? Who are the people to ask? Which organisations can really help? This chapter will attempt to answer these and related questions.

The company's objectives, aims, corporate plan and area of activity

Clearly it is important, first, to note down certain facts about the company in relation to its objectives, aims, corporate plan and area of activity. The following checklist will provide a starting point.

1.   *The company's business is:* (note details: manufacturing/distribution/ retailing and give area of production or service)
2.   *The company operates from:* (give details of nature of premises, plant, etc., and location)
3.   *The company operates through:* (give details of type of operation, identifying the different stages and/or links in the chain)
4.   *The company's constitution is:* (give details of constitution (limited company, plc, etc.), type of organisation, UK or international, ownership, shareholdings, management and decision-making, etc.)
5.   *The company's objectives, aims, corporate plan, activities and sphere of operation are:* (give relevant information and state whether UK, national or regional, whether operating in continental Europe, or international, specifying countries involved)
6.   *The company sees its present purpose as* (employing people, or fulfilling a market, or developing technology, etc.)
7.   *The company sees its conceivable evolution into the future as* (long-term targets and strategies).

Surprisingly, many organisations and companies do not have a document setting out their 'inner' thoughts like this. To them, such an exercise may seem difficult, or irrelevant, or something to be pigeonholed until there is time available. However, this is a sort of 'job description' for the organisation. It is as important to be clear as to what the organisation is and does, as it is to be clear about the type of staff who are needed to work in it.

Components of good corporate citizenship

Good corporate citizenship can be simply enshrined in the single word 'response'. Company response to outside conditions, outside opinions, outside trends, internal considerations, including staff and related priorities – this is really what it is all about. Initiative enables a company to think ahead, anticipate, and be *pro*active rather than, as is so often the case, *re*active or, worse still, reactionary, in its responses.

In corporate communications, now increasingly recognised as an important management tool, emphasis is placed on the many and diverse messages the company feeds its numerous target audiences. Their number, adequacy and effectiveness are planned, including 'tone of voice', nature of delivery, whether in the form of letter, or display advertising, on television, or in print. Good corporate citizenship includes evaluating and using the 'mirror image', as information coming from outside into the company – that is the company's responses to the messages it receives from others. These messages are continually reaching the company. The extent to which they are recognised, analysed, acted upon and used – to the better fulfilment of company objectives – will be related to the extent to which the company can consider that it is a good corporate citizen.

Response

So how does the company look at its 'response'?

This can be expressed as follows:

- RESPONSIBILITY. The company's responsibility to determine its mission and its overall role, and to ensure the ethical standards to which it works.
- EFFECTIVENESS. The company's effectiveness in bringing its products and/or services to the market economically and cost-effectively.

- SCOPE. The company's recognition of the scope of its areas of operation and influence.
- PRECISION. The company's precision in defining its messages, their consistency and their relevance to reputation and the overall enterprise.
- OBJECTIVITY. The company's objectivity in determining the emphasis put on messages it transmits to its different target audiences.
- KNOWLEDGE. The company's overall knowledge of, intelligence of and data-collection systems on future trends and likely developments in the marketplace, and also in wider spheres.
- SENSITIVITY. The company's sensitivity to assess the implications of its actions today and their relevance to the future, over wider horizons of time and area.
- EVALUATION. The company's ability to conduct objective evaluation to determine levels of progress achieved.

The importance of good reputation

At Board and working management levels, the company's attention should be focused on recognising the importance of reputation – for its products or services, its role in the community, as an employer, for example. In the narrow and immediate context, the company can easily recognise the advantages of a good reputation. These can be summarised as follows:

- Others will be more willing to consider the company's viewpoint.
- The company will find it easier to recruit and motivate staff.
- The good reputation of the company will enhance and add value to the company's products and/or services.
- The company reputation will be reflected in a better share price if it is a public company.
- The company, strengthening its information structure with the society in which it operates, improves resources in all areas – from staff to technology and customers.

What goes into creating a good reputation?

Very simply, there are three components to a company's reputation. These are the behaviour of the company itself; how the company communicates on the issues affecting it; and the consequent interactions of these with each other.

The freedoms which result from a good reputation

The company with a good reputation gains considerable freedom of action. It will be automatically trusted to have responsible policies because society values its initiatives and soundness. For this important reason, the company must ensure that it has recognised the need to conduct itself in accordance with its own company code of business ethics. This should have been properly thought through and agreed at Board and working management levels.

Furthermore, it is important that the code of business ethics to which the company works is understood and welcomed as well as promulgated widely, both inside and outside the company, at all levels.

Finding out where the company stands

Given the increased attention and emphasis being awarded to business ethics today, it is all the more important for the company to know where it stands in this overall area. The first step in finding out is to collect existing information and analyse it to determine what sort of gaps, if any, exist. The following checklist should be helpful.

1. Is the company mission statement up to date and relevant? Does it indicate that there is an existing company code of practice and/or business ethics, relevant to employees, shareholders, customers, legislators and the community? Is the mission statement (probably condensed) understood in its markets? How is this monitored?
2. Does the company have a system for discussing corporate responsibility at all management levels?
3. Who is responsible for ethics and corporate responsibility in the company at Board level, and at working management levels? (There may be several responsible, depending on the size and type of company and the ethical factors involved. Issues in sales ethics, for example, will differ from those in technology or personnel relations. What is needed is a structure of leadership from the Board through to the shop floor.)
4. What is the company record in effective research and development? Is it better than that of competitors? Is it good enough to keep up with its future markets? Is it being properly monitored?
5. Does the company contribute to the local community? How?
   - In terms of money?
   - In terms of work on community projects?

15

- In terms of education and training?
- In terms of sponsorship or charitable support?
- Is the extent of this effort increasing?
- For how long has this effort been made and/or is it ongoing or project-based?

6. Who has responsibility for safety, pollution and environmental matters within the company at Board level, and at working management levels?

7. Does the company have a policy in the areas of sponsorship and charitable giving? Which sorts of projects are supported? Who are the decision-makers? What level of support is given – in cash or in kind?

8. Is the level of charitable and/or sponsorship support stable? Increasing?

9. Does the company have a formal procedure to deal with customer or supplier complaints? How is this organised? Who is responsible for this function? Does the Board get regular reports?

10. Does the company commission regular tracking surveys on company image and in relation to specific issues? In which sectors? How often? How does it compare against the competition?

11. Does the company play its full part in the affairs of its local community, of its business sector, and of its industry overall? How?

12. Are quality control and assurance procedures in place in relevant areas? Have they been monitored and/or updated within the past year? Does the company support the British Standards Institution's Quality Assurance Programmes (BS 5750 and its associated standards)?

13. Does the company *care* for its present and past employees? How? Has its policy been monitored, and/or updated recently?

14. What methods of communication does the company use to ensure that there is an even, two-way flow of communication between the Board and employees?

15. Does the company's annual report reflect the company's record and activities as a good corporate citizen?

16. Does the company have adequate and effective communications systems related to the following areas:
- The media?
- Trade and professional?
- Community?
- Government?
- Business?

- Environment?
- City and financial?

17. How does the company rate understanding its performance in the following key areas of the environment:
    - Solid waste?
    - Water?
    - Air?
    - Noise?
    - Biosphere generally?

18. Does the company have a share-ownership scheme for its employees? How does this measure up against current practice?

19. Does the company help its employees understand matters affecting them personally, such as money management, health and safety, and development skills?

20. Does the company have a policy of acknowledging personal effort – both in the company and in the wider more personal sense?

21. Does the company operate a programme of regular communications with:
    - Shareholders?
    - Financial analysts?
    - Relevant fund managers?

The company and its commercial and industrial infrastructure

Where the company stands depends not only on the company itself but also on the commercial and industrial infrastructure with which it is related, and of which it forms part. Two distinct, but interrelated types of infrastructure can contribute to good corporate citizenship, and both can interreact with local, national, and supranational government infrastructures.

The 'home environment'

The first is the infrastructure that a company creates as a 'home environment' within and around itself. That of companies in the BAT group forms a good example. The BAT case history (see Appendix I) gives a view of a few of the many instances where companies in the group resonate with the societies around them to continuing mutual benefit. Food security, help to local engineering industry, health education, and local culture all figure in projects apparently quite unconnected with the basic activities of the companies concerned. These are local opportunities and initiatives for worthwhile paternalism co-ordinated and orchestrated from the top. That way consistency of approach and practicality in outcome are encouraged. The results benefit local society and improving society benefits national and company development. It is immaterial whether such initiatives are motivated by religious considerations (IBM, Tata, Cadbury) or by a humanistic approach perhaps deriving from the influence of Robert Owen (Shell, BP, ICI, BAT). Such companies can find themselves leaders in the communities, providing leadership far beyond the narrow confines of commerce and business, and sometimes being effective and benevolent mainstays of whole countries.

The 'local environment'

The other main type of infrastructure or environment is the local one, where the company takes part in activities not so much in the role of leader as along with other companies for their general mutual benefit. This can take different forms, and trade associations, professional institutions, co-operative research bodies and institutions, multi-client surveys, co-operative development projects, and neighbourhoods such as the Raleigh-Durham Research Triangle in the USA, or science parks in Britain, are all forms of industry–society infrastructure.

An interesting example on a small scale is the West Greater London Productivity Association. This was begun by four individuals heeding a government initiative; it developed with the encouragement of a quango, the British Productivity Council; and it became self-propelled as a registered charity in 1972. Supported at the time entirely by local firms, it became a not-for-profit company to promote industry and commerce, to hold meetings and training courses, to provide information, advice and publications, and to further research and investigation. It covers a wide spectrum, from low to high technology, large and small industrial and commercial firms and individuals, public as well as private enterprise, local authority interests, and further and higher education.

That sort of mutual self- and community help is good corporate citizenship. Practical ethics is good business in cases like this because the understanding of people who work in the companies as well as of their customers, is improved; and because member firms often make components for, or provide goods or services to, other member firms – and the higher the quality of such components, goods and services, the better for both seller and buyer firms.

In conclusion

- Finding out where the company stands is not difficult.
- It is possible that the current company effort may be spread too widely and lack focus. The areas to look at are indicated in this chapter.
- Taking the time and trouble to analyse the situation today, to make changes as necessary, to provide focus, and to monitor progress is well worthwhile.
- Planning to get the resultant message across more effectively in the company can enhance turnover and profit.

CHAPTER 3

Setting an ethical framework for business

This chapter deals with the broad spectrum of ethics in business, identifying the key areas of concern and giving guidance on the priorities for both the present and the future.

Cynicism

A fair dose of cynicism in business is fit and proper. It is, however, unfortunately the case that some businesses overdo this. For example, there has been much media coverage of the cynical approach of some businesses to the emerging 'green' markets. Only too often one can be offered the new 'green' or 'ozone friendly' version of a spray, detergent or other cleaning agent, and even a new 'organic' food or investment product (the so-called 'ethical fund'). Mostly these products are offered at a premium, for which no rationale, let alone evidence, is provided.

Another example of corporate cynicism is the increasing trend for companies to issue smart glossy brochures citing their performance on corporate responsibility. These brochures often look very sophisticated and reflect substantial investment in terms of time and money. But in their use of resources they hardly, if ever, actually reflect the very issue they are intended to promote! The company committed to a policy of good corporate citizenship will recognise the value of the information to be imparted and the need to do this in a simple, cost-effective manner which in itself will underline the fact that the policy is in place. In other words, it will follow a policy of 'fewer words, more meaning', perhaps including the information in the company Annual Report, and, if it does produce a special brochure, ensuring that the resources used are husbanded carefully and thoughtfully.

Practice

Printed below is a selection of statements from professional institutions, trade organisations and companies, which, broadly, fall into the area of practice. In essence they cover the area of 'vision' statements (declarations of intent by company management on policy and aspirations), 'mission' statements (agreed company policy, principles and targets), codes of practice (agreed practices by which the organisation stands, procedures to be followed in relation to enquiry and complaint, together with explanations on sanctions to be used if the organisation fails to honour its code of practice), and codes of business ethics (the moral principles by which the company stands).

The 'vision' statement

The vision statement sets out the way ahead as the company sees it. It declares where the management wants to place future development, where its aspirations lie. This example comes from the Midland Bank and was presented to staff at the bank's national sales conference. At that conference Michael Fuller, Chief Executive, UK Banking, said:

What do I mean by a vision? And what is its value? Let's look first at the wider world. We're not by any means the only company which has faced or is facing change on major scale. The same conditions have been experienced in many other businesses.

British Airways, Marks & Spencer, MacDonald's. They're all recognised as leaders and innovators in very different fields. But what do they have in common? In a word, I suggest, *unity*. [They are] businesses which have managed change in the most positive way. We have a unity, a sense of purpose and commitment, a set of goals that everyone in the company can share, and understand and commit to. In other words, [we have] a clear vision, a belief in the direction and aims of the company. Not only that, but when the customer recognises that vision, too, and becomes part of it you know you've got it right. We've spent a lot of time in seeking to develop a vision for Midland. We think we've succeeded. The first test for us is your acceptance of that vision, that mission statement. It didn't emerge haphazardly, without heat and light, some anguish, discussion and debate into the night. But ultimately the team here today came to a unanimous determination. In four words, we want Midland to become 'Britain's most recommended Bank' because we are reliable; we are responsive; we are honest; we listen and we care; we look professional; and we are a modern bank.

We are going to get there by: customer specialisation into two sales streams (consumer and corporate) and one processing stream; investment of capital and management resources into technology, training, products, premises [and] positioning; establishment of service standards and to meet specified needs of internal [and] external customers; [and] clear definitions of responsibility and accountability reflected in the objectives of each member of the business.

This statement is simple and direct. It gives all members of staff a clear idea of where they stand.

The 'mission' statement

A mission statement sets out where the company stands here and now. It is the expression of agreed company policy, principles and targets. This example comes from Radio Rentals, a member of the Thorn-EMI group. The company has a long record of service and currently speaks for some 1.5 million customers who rent television sets, and increasingly other products, too, including major 'white goods' (dishwashers, washing machines and the like). The company is in touch with some 80,000 customers every day. Recent developments have led to a re-evaluation of the importance of service, always a high priority with this company. The new 'Total Service' concept guarantees that the company's service personnel will be available to the customer 24 hours a day, 365 days a year. The customer also has a say in the timing of service visits.

RADIO RENTALS

- **Our mission**
To be the customer's first choice for quality product and service packages provided through flexible value added rental deals.

- **Our business**
We believe quality in our products and services is fundamental to achieving long lasting relationships with our customers.

We will offer a wide range of rental propositions, with the flexibility to meet a variety of customer requirements.

Retail products will be used to augment the main rental business.

We will produce a financial performance which attracts investment into the Company.

- **Our company**
Our outlook will be modern, stylish and forward looking.

Our shops will be enticing, vital places, where customers are encouraged to explore an exciting range of advanced products.

Customers will experience us as warm, friendly and helpful people who always keep promises.

- **Our people**
We are committed to establishing an open working style:

where everyone is aware of our goals and objectives, and can involve themselves in the affairs of the Company;

where individuals are valued, and take pride in being a member of the Radio Rentals team;

in which people can realise their potential and earn the rewards for high individual performance.

Again, this is a tightly drawn mission statement which is reflected at all levels in detailed corporate plans.

The industry customer code

An industry customer code is the expression of the standards to which the industry is expected to perform. Such codes are, in the main, voluntary, frequently worked out by the leading trade association in the field and in consultation with the Office of Fair Trading. Naturally they relate to the organisations in membership of the trade association which is, of course, powerless to assist dissatisfied consumers when the company complained about is not in membership. They are promulgated widely and the relevant simple explanatory leaflets generally contain a step-by-step guide on how to complain, together with a note of the sanctions which can be activated if there has been a breach of the code.

The example is taken from the unit trust industry, where a new customer code has been developed by the Unit Trust Association, with the help of the UTA Customer Standards Committee (see Appendix II). This includes strong representation by independent experts and leaders of consumer opinion. The code reflects the fact that, under the provisions of the Financial Services Act, it is still important for an industry to identify 'good corporate citizenship' and 'add value', ensuring that the good reputation of the specific industry is protected and enhanced by the industry trade association on behalf of the member companies in the industry. In so doing an effective industry customer code serves both the industry and the consumers/customers. The UTA customer code is promulgated widely both by the UTA itself, and by member companies.

The code of business ethics

Very few companies, alas, appear to have a formal code of ethics. There is some evidence that action is starting to take place, but it is little and late. (The initiative of the International Association of Business Communicators is to be welcomed. Its code of ethics is featured in Appendix II.)

The following is the model statement and code as promulgated by the Institute of Business Ethics which was inaugurated in 1986. Among its patrons and Council members are an impressive number of British business leaders. The Institute seeks to clarify ethical issues in business, to propose positive solutions to problems and to establish common ground with people of goodwill of all faiths. Its funds have charitable status.

Model statement and code

The responsibility of the whole board
The Institute makes the point that an analysis of a number of company statements and codes can provide a framework from which a company can develop its own individual statement or produce a code of ethics. It stresses that it is important that this is not left to an enthusiast on the Board or delegated to the personnel manager but is seen as part of the responsibility of the whole Board. It identifies the fact that model business codes have existed for a number of years, and notes that those of the British Institute of Management and of the Christian Association of Business Executives have been widely used. There are also international codes; an oil company for instance has adopted the OECD Guidelines for International Investment and Multinational Enterprise as its statement of business principles.

Introduction by the Chairman
The Institute recommends that an outline of a Model Statement of Business Principles should start with a preface or introduction signed by the Chairman or Chief Executive Officer of the company, or both. It states: 'Start with a sentence on the purpose of the Statement – mention the values which are important to the top management in the conduct of the business, such as integrity, efficiency, professionalism and responsibility. Set out the role of the company in the community and end with a personal endorsement of the Statement and the expectation that the standard set out in it will be maintained by all involved in the organisation. Date the Preface.'
Key areas to include:

(a) The object of the Business – The service which is being provided, financial objectives, and the business's role in society as the company sees it.
(b) Customer relations – The importance of customer satisfaction and good faith in all agreements. The priority given to customer needs, fair pricing and after-sales service.
(c) Stakeholders (Shareholders or other providers of money) – The protection of investment made in the company and proper 'return' on money lent. A commitment to effective communication with this group of people.
(d) Suppliers – Long term co-operation. Prompt settling of bills. Joint actions to achieve quality and efficiency.
(e) Employees – How the business values employees. The company's policies on: recruitment, organisation, development and training, rewards, communication, work conditions, health and safety, industrial relationships, equal employment opportunity, retirement, severence and redundancy.
(f) Society or the wider community – Compliance with the spirit of laws as well

as the letter. The company's obligations to conform to environmental and safety standards. The involvement of the Company and its staff in local affairs. The corporate policy on giving to education and charities. The leadership role of the business in maintaining high standards both within the organisation and in its dealings with others.

(g) Other matters – Relations with competitors, research and development policy and management responsibility. The ethical standards expected of employees. (This is best covered in a separate statement addressed primarily to employees.)

Key points to remember in drafting a code of business ethics

- To be effective and understood by all employees, a specific code of business ethics should be relatively short and written in simple language. Ideally it should be concerned with problems experienced by employees and include something about procedures to be followed when confronted with an ethical dilemma at work. It should also make clear what will happen if the code is breached.
- The introduction should be a statement on the reason why the code has been produced and its status, e.g., that it applies to all employees and that any non-compliance will be considered a serious disciplinary matter.
- Conflicts of interest should be covered. These should include a clause covering possible conflicts of interest such as personal interest (or that of an immediate member of the family) in an organisation with which the company does business, which could lead to perceptions of self-interested behaviour. This interest could include directorship, employment of close family members or a significant shareholding. A directive that all such potential conflicts should be reported to the employees's immediate superior and recorded should also be included. A ban on share dealing as a result of information obtained in the course of work for the organisation is another key area for inclusion.
- Specific guidance on the giving or receiving of cash, goods, services, hospitality or bribes in any form should be covered. A statement should be included that all offers made to employees of anything that might be construed as an inducement shall not be accepted. Company policy on the offering of gifts to others and the level of hospitality that it is acceptable to offer or receive (this excludes small 'goodwill' gifts exchanged at Christmas (diaries, etc.)) should be covered. Direction should be included that any gifts offered or received should be reported to a superior and recorded. The fact that it applies equally to business with overseas customers and suppliers and should be subject to auditors' inspection should be noted; also the fact that business entertainment should be on a reciprocal basis and on a scale consistent with the status of the employee in the organisation.
- Duties of confidentiality should be spelt out – Where applicable a statement should be included that information which is obtained in the course of work is the property of the company. The fact that it must not be disclosed to unauthorised persons and that this also applies when the employee is no longer working for the organisation should be included. Steps to be taken to safeguard information which is of value to competitors or others should be identified.
- Standards for the working environment of employees and the effect of business activity on the local community should be included. Also a statement that the

health and safety of employees and others involved with the business is of paramount importance and that staff are responsible for seeing that the products and operations not only comply with the legal requirements but take into account the well-being of the general public especially those living in the vicinity of manufacturing plants.

• Equal Employment Opportunity should be spelt out – including an undertaking that selection for a position in the company shall be based on suitability for the job and that there shall be no discrimination purely on grounds of race, religion, marital status, sex, colour, nationality, disability or ethnic or national origin. Similar undertakings should be given relevant to promotion and security of employment.

Other areas which could be covered could include: political activities by individuals; obligations under competition or anti-trust laws; 'moonlighting' by employees; sexual harassment.

Finally, The Institute of Business Ethics stresses that for a Code of Conduct or Business Ethics to be effective, it must be developed from within the company, albeit making use of a model and the experience of others.

Production and application of statements and codes
The statement of company philosophy and/or code of Business Ethics is important, but equally important are the questions of how it is developed, how presented and used. Of particular importance, perhaps, is what happens if it is not followed and what mechanisms there are for changing and adding to it.

Beginning – There are many ways to begin on such an exercise. Obvious ones are: the Annual Report; induction of new employees; setting up a special group chaired by a Non-Executive Director of the company. It is, however, obvious and important that employees at all levels need to be drawn into the consultation process. It is essential for a common commitment to emerge. This in time gives the new Code its credentials of authenticity, internally and externally, and adds to the respect with which it is universally viewed.

Presentation – When the new code has been drafted it is important that it is checked through for legal and other relevant implications. Its promulgation then becomes a matter for thought, consideration and implementation. It is self-evident that copies of the new code should be given to all employees. It should also be promulgated more widely, to all the target audiences of the company, including the media. Its presentation can be organised to be formal (through the arrangement of special meetings, briefings, etc.) or informal (by distribution through the post or being reprinted in relevant company newspapers and reports).

Monitoring the code – This should be through the organisation of a group (preferably at high executive level, chaired by a Non-Executive Director of the company) meeting to discuss and report on the operation of the code at regular intervals. This body should also be given the responsibility of updating the code to take in modifications which appear necessary once the code has been working over a period.

Breaches of the code – This is always the awkward area. It is self-evident that there should be a process indicating what should be done in the case of a violation of the code. The process is then simple and straightforward: the facts need to be reviewed and the circumstances considered. If there is found to be a breach the matter should be referred to an identified and more senior level within the company. When the matter has been thoroughly reviewed and the breach has been confirmed, then the sanctions already agreed should be imposed. Any person or persons found to be guilty must be disciplined appropriately if the code is to retain credibility.

The sensitive areas

There are several sensitive areas which the company should consider in deciding to inaugurate a Code of Business Ethics. The company position on all of these should be known and agreed. Whether or not they are matters for inclusion in the Code is for Board decision.

The sensitive areas include:

To what extent the company should be involved with nations whose politics are regarded as alien to the majority of company employees and probably shareholders.

Whether or not the company should adopt a policy of positive discrimination in job selection.

Just how far a company should go in securing contracts which will provide sustained employment for its workforce but would involve a break of its normal codes of conduct.

These, then, are the fundamental considerations which a company should consider in contemplating the overall area of vision statements, mission statements, statements of company philosophy and codes of business ethics. It is to be hoped that it will now be easier for the reader to enable a code to be drafted suitable for a particular company and tailored to the needs of that particular company.

Ways ahead are clear, and initiative and common purpose are both required for progress and must go ahead hand in hand. There is much good precedent, and it is up to people in companies, individually and collectively, to look around them and make their work more efficient and effective. In this context, the role of the non-executive director has much to commend it, both in relation to the development of company codes and in wider spheres. The independence of this person means that he or she brings to the boardroom a level of objectivity when examining the specific issues involved which is, in itself, a valuable contribution to the company. Selection of the right mix for the non-executive directors to serve the Board can provide most valuable and cost-effective resources for the company. It is, naturally, most important for the chairman and chief executive to resist the temptation to people the Board with non-executive 'yes' men and women who will be permissive and deliver the supporting votes as and when needed!

Thus the company is in a good position to develop good corporate citizenship and should find that sensible ethics is good for business.

Short-term quick profit at the expense of society benefits only the profiteer. The company and its environments exist in symbiosis and ideally both should develop in efficiency synergistically. The long-term good of the one is in the long-term good of the other.

In conclusion

- There are many examples of company mission statements, codes and similar documents to point the way forward for the reader (see Part V: Appendices).
- Codes of business ethics are increasingly important. They can be most important in helping the company achieve its corporate objectives.
- A code of business ethics is not a cosmetic option. It must be drafted with the knowledge, commitment and involvement of the whole Board of the company and in consultation with all employees.
- The process for monitoring the code, examining possible breaches and undertaking any necessary disciplinary action should be clearly identified.
- The role of the non-executive directors of the company in this area is an important one.
- The promulgation of the code offers the company many opportunities for positive initiatives. The code should be circulated to all employees, shareholders, suppliers and the media. (Note: the author acknowledges the use of source material from *Company Philosophies and Codes of Business Ethics*, published by The Institute of Business Ethics (1988).)
- The company should resonate with its local environments, and particularly with local people.
- Good company ethics is the practical approach to sensible overall company management. The so-called moral concerns of society can be a realistic basis for doing a job well, so that the company and its various types of environment all thrive to their mutual collective benefit. Widely recognised 'good manufacturing practices' have been used in productive industry for many years. They result in better business and improved profit. Good company ethics is the non-technological counterpart.
- Different types of detailed principle or rule can be derived for different types of company in different industries and circumstances, but the code of good company ethics should include:

- Providing value to the customer.
- Value derived by the worker, manager and investor from the effort or resource supplied.
- Sensible use of raw materials, efficient processing and minimising waste.
- Learning from industrial activity and development so that industrial evolution is in harmony with evolution of the human and natural world.
- Seeing and thinking widely around and ahead of the immediate situation so that what is done provides a reasoned stage for progress into the future.

CHAPTER 4

The role of leadership in achieving good corporate citizenship

One of the most readable new books on the subject of leadership in business is *Making It Happen* by Sir John Harvey-Jones. While not the primary purpose of Sir John's book, the importance of good corporate citizenship and the need for business ethics are evident in every word he writes. It is because he recognises the wider responsibilities of business and has acted accordingly throughout his business life that his reputation at ICI and in his many other business roles has been polished to such a high degree of excellence. The weight he gives his carefully chosen words on the subject of leadership certainly provides the aspiring business leader with essential reading.

In his book Sir John says:

Although I am convinced that the prime management problem is 'making it happen', one has to accept that in life there is always at least an even chance that one is going the wrong way. Not only is it extremely easy to go the wrong way, and indeed many businesses have foundered on the basis of one, usually inadvertent, mistaken direction, but all of us are aware that a lot of businesses aren't going anywhere at all.

This chapter, therefore, looks at where the company is going, the part played by initiative and the role of leadership within the company in the establishment of a reputation and record as a good corporate citizen. Hopefully it will guide the reader on how to spot areas of opportunity and how to develop these to best effect.

Priorities for the aspiring business leader

The aspiring business leader must possess a strong sense of self-awareness. This includes a deep understanding of his or her personal qualities – for instance, attitude to challenge and risk – as well as such matters as strength of commitment to and pride in the company.

Important, too, is the recognition that a leader can sometimes be very lonely, frequently has to take much unjustified criticism, rarely is 'loved', and often is considered 'tricky', 'difficult' or perhaps 'bloody-minded'. This is only to be expected. A leader, after all, has a vision; he or she can see further into the future and has a wider horizon than others. It is natural for these others to be nervous, worried, upset even, that their faculties do not allow them to keep pace with the leader. Any aspiring business leader worried by this must take a long hard look at his or her aspirations!

Next, the aspiring business leader should take a detailed look at his or her ambitions for the company. Today it is recognised that the company has a 'living' personality. Many specialist research firms will monitor how that personality evolves over time; some will even give it a 'human dimension'. They will tell you that the company is male or female; old or young; working-, middle- or 'yuppy'-class! The leader must recognise that it is important for him or her to have a sharp, crisp, clear idea of the profile and personality of the company. Then it will be easier to develop company identity and to come to conclusions about how that identity should evolve over time and the objectives, in terms of reputation and business targets, to be reached over given periods of time.

Finally, our aspirant business leader must recognise clearly that what will be achieved directly relates to his or her contribution to the company, to the level of commitment, clarity, determination and accurate targetting of all business operations which stem from his or her leadership. It is also important to realise that 'the buck stops here'!

Planning the way ahead

Business is exciting and the person who can have the most exciting time of all is the person who manages the company, plans its way ahead, and leads it. There are many possible paths to choose from – choosing the right one can be great fun; following it and ensuring that all difficulties in the way of the company's development are overcome can provide enormous challenges. The sense of purpose and achievement when goals are met is exhilarating, to say the least.

The strange fact is that in all the tomes written about management, in all the classes at which management skills are taught, so little time and effort is spent in relating the functions and roles to the human aspects of challenge, excitement and achievement.

One of the most impressive business leaders on this subject is Peter Benton, Director General of the British Institute of Management. He explains it simply in terms of the man or woman who is 'larger than life', with the sense of exuberance and fun which 'spills over' to enable contributions to be made in many other areas. These can include the areas of the community, the arts, the local charity, the newly formed 'worthy cause', and so on. Peter Benton goes on to talk about how, over time, business leaders with these qualities of leadership have made their very significant contributions to society at large. Going right back to the Renaissance, in cities like Florence and Rome, extremely successful individuals demonstrated their success by commissioning works of art. Again, as Peter Benton puts it: 'In the thirties, in Chicago, one of the most aggressively commercial cities in the world, the love of private and public clients for top world-class architecture and for the innovators still remains there as evidence to their success.'

There are numerous other examples of the leaders who have contributed to society over the centuries. And very welcome they were, too – appreciated by the society at large and the source of great pride to large numbers of ordinary people, citizens of the particular cities they enriched in many ways.

A popular theme in management books is that of planning, dealing with problems, setting the strategic direction, analysing it, identifying the competitive advantage, assessing its value and so on. Advice abounds and is there for the asking. Sometimes, though, there is so much waffle that it is difficult to recognise the real 'nuts', the acorns of wisdom which tend to be well hidden!

So, what should our aspirant business leader be looking for when setting the course for the way ahead? Clearly, first, it is important to know where the company stands today, as well as where it has come from.

Next, it is important to know where the company needs to go and whether any change of direction or emphasis is needed. In looking at this area it needs to be recognised that the company has a 'living' personality, that it is constantly changing and developing and that this will continue – endlessly.

Another fundamental fact which needs both to be recognised and to be given the high priority it deserves, is that the company exists in society alongside its competitors. As much as possible needs to be known about their activities and gleaned about their planning for the future. In this connection, it is not as difficult as may be thought to create a barometer on competitors' activities. There is much well-informed financial analysis of companies and the directions in which they are going. One simple, cost-effective and fast method I have used to good effect over the years works like this:

1. Identify the, say, three key competitors the company wishes to monitor.
2. Commission press cuttings on the companies over a given period of time, say, three months.
3. Commission a leading independent media specialist in the area of trade or industry concerned to write a confidential independent report which brings together:

    (a) his or her evaluation of the press coverage of the competitors against similar press coverage on the company (with access to the relevant information);
    (b) his or her evaluation of the progress being made by each organisation. If the media specialist is well regarded in the industry they will be knowledgeable about movements of key executives within the companies, new appointments, important events which have taken place during the period being reviewed, significant additions to plant and equipment, new products which may be in the process of being developed, and so on.

4. Set the parameters for the report and, when it is received, hold a review meeting with the independent specialist.
5. Hold an internal meeting to review the report with colleagues, and use its content as appropriate in setting the way ahead for the company.
6. In considering the above, it should be recognised that the objective of the company must be to be considered the best in its field of activity, with the highest possible reputation for excellence, and a good corporate citizen.

In setting the way ahead it is vital never to forget that business involves taking risks, and that the business which does not take risks is going nowhere. The level of acceptable risk is the key question to be addressed. Getting this right sorts out the sheep from the lambs!

Making things happen

There is no mystique in making things happen. It needs sound common sense and mature judgement. An aspirant business leader will know that there are two types of leader – the leader who leads from the front (the autocrat) and the leader who leads from the back (the man or woman who strives hard for consensus, for agreement), who (wisely or not) plays down the element of leadership.

Anyone who is or has been a leader will know that the job calls for two other talents and abilities in large measures. The first of these is true grit, determination to make things happen. The second, surprisingly perhaps, is physical stamina. The ability to stay up late and to work for long hours without a break is almost universally present in leaders. Those who are not blessed with physical toughness have to make up for its loss in other ways – and hard they must find it, too.

Spotting areas of opportunity and developing these to best effect

This is perhaps the most difficult area in which to judge whether or not qualities of leadership are present. The true leader has a 'leader's nose' – an intuition, a hunch, a sixth sense which points to where the new opportunity may lie, where the new challenge can be created, where the difficulties may be lurking. Some may say that this is just 'luck', and maybe it is. What is certain is that it is a unique and most valuable quality and it is important to recognise whether and to what extent it is present.

Excellence and good corporate citizenship

Excellence, so long considered a dirty word, must be recognised as a virtue. In today's business climate, no company should ever accept second best, for to do so is to abrogate responsibility in business. In the role of leadership, the leader must always search for excellence and quality – of premises, of processes, of services, of raw materials, of people, of suppliers, customers, shareholders, and so on. In particular, he or she must strive for excellence in himself or herself. Standards need to be set for every sector of business, but arguably the most important standard of all is the one set for oneself – both in private and in business life.

The good corporate citizen recognises all of this, and puts in place policies to find and preserve excellence in the everyday practice of business.

It is, after all, the collective results of our individual actions that make all the difference in the world. The leader strives to enlist the help of each and every member of his or her team in making that difference.

In conclusion

- Leadership is important if a company is to be a good corporate citizen.
- Leadership is not solely the preserve of the boss of the firm. Indeed, leadership qualities should be present in many if not most of the company's employees and associates. Such a company is rich indeed.

- Leadership calls for certain qualities of which determination, grit and physical stamina are three important ones.
- Leadership is about seeking and finding excellence in all the areas of the company's operations, and encouraging and preserving these important qualities.
- Leadership is about persuading others that their individual actions can make all the difference in the world, and leading by example in this context.

PART II

The key areas – contributions from the experts

CHAPTER 5

The company and its marketing policy

DR ELIZABETH NELSON
Chairman, Taylor Nelson Group

The market in which a firm supplies goods or services is (or should be) a direct beneficiary of the firm's activities. To supply that market well is one aspect of good corporate citizenship, and there are many facets of this.

To market effectively in the future, particularly after the emergence of the single European market, it is important to understand the influences of recent years. It is also important to appreciate the implications for the future.

This chapter examines the overall position.

Security and status

The period of the late 1940s and 1950s in Europe was one of strong commitment to the work ethic. It was a period not only of physical rebuilding but also of rebuilding democratic structures. Only through hard work could economic and social security be achieved. This was a period when success was increasingly measured by the value of the status symbols owned: how your home was decorated, the number of modern labour-saving devices you possessed, and the type of car you drove. Unlike that in United States, the mood in Europe was less one of optimism than of determination to dig a way out of the hole. Technology was seen as a benevolent force leading to increased material prosperity, and at the same time freeing people from the drudgery of work. The reactions against this set of values among the younger, post-war generation in the late 1960s and 1970s were profound and far-reaching.

This chapter is based on a lecture to the Royal Society of Arts in November 1988.

Personal expression and consumerism

Anti-authority, the demand for individuality and personal expression, held sway in the late 1960s and early 1970s. Protest trends such as consumer scepticism, return to nature, rejection of the benefits of technology, equal opportunities for women, anti-bigness, anti-industry, were all reflections of rebellion against industrial society values. Out of this protest movement grew consumerism, a feeling that a production-led industrial society did not give the consumer a fair deal.

The impact of these trends since the 1960s has been profound and the protest movement has given way to an assimilation of these values throughout society. The mid- and late 1980s were another watershed. The important new changes in social values will have an impact on society well into the twenty-first century.

Pleasure as a right, not as a reward

To earlier generations faced with the need to work long hours in arduous conditions, pleasure was seen as a reward which had to be earned. Since the 1960s, there has been a major change in this attitude, particularly among young people in Europe. The pursuit of pleasure is increasingly regarded as a legitimate objective, as a part of the development of a full life. This has dramatically reduced people's tolerance for boring or physically arduous work. Unless it is intrinsically interesting, work is no longer seen as a necessary or morally valuable activity.

Closely allied to the pursuit of pleasure is the desire for emotional experience. People have the need to feel their bodies in new and different intensive ways, the desire for frequent emotional experiences and the enjoyment of doing something which is just a little dangerous or forbidden.

These trends have had dramatic effects on the everyday life of Europeans, with the rapid growth of all kinds of labour-saving devices not only at work, but also at home and in leisure activities. For large sections of the population there has been an increased willingness to trade off product advantages for additional convenience. Examples of this are non-iron fabrics, convenience foods and the use of microwave ovens. These trends have also contributed to a wider use of fast food outlets, which completely eliminate the need for meal preparation. With people reacting strongly against situations which they regard as time-wasting or boring, the level of waiting which people are prepared to tolerate has diminished.

With the demise of the Cartesian model of man as a rational being separated from animals at least partly because of his reliance on the senses of sight and sound, we now have the model of man who savours each of his senses (preferably all at the same time). To the consumer, this means the joy of smelling fresh bread and newly ground coffee, feeling silk next to one's skin or enjoying the texture of a ripe brie.

Coming to terms with technology and the environment

In the 1950s and early 1960s technology was seen as the key to future progress. It would free man from the demand for arduous physical work and boring repetitive tasks and bring a whole range of consumer goods within the purchasing power of most of the population. People were fascinated with the romance of technology, with the incredible range of things which could be achieved through technological progress. That was the era of the gadget, where a product was judged on how technically advanced it was, rather than on its function.

In the late 1960s and early 1970s a reaction set in, with people rejecting what they saw as an impersonal, technologically driven world, in favour of a back-to-nature movement and of a simpler lifestyle which, it was believed, was enjoyed in earlier pre-technology generations. In its most extreme form, this led to the hippie communes, but it was also responsible for the success of products made from natural ingredients, whether it be shampoo with lanolin from sheep's wool, or the Campaign for Real Ale, or Hovis's nostalgic 1930s advertising campaign. It was also the period when people reacted against plastic, the time of the scrubbed pine country kitchens.

Today's societal evolution involves the development and maturing of two very important and conflicting trends in European attitudes to technology. On the one hand, there is an increasing acceptance of products which, although not naturally based, perform functions which cannot be done by their natural counterparts. Products are judged not so much on their composition as on their usefulness. This is associated with a demand for 'user-friendly' products which not only fulfil useful functions but also are easy to use. The user is less interested in the microchip that performs the function and more interested in what the product can actually do, how easy it is to operate. This can already be seen very clearly in the consumer resistance to complicated instructions, procedures and computer programs. Two of the key limiting factors on the use of home computers at present are the need to show clear consumer benefits and the demand for user-friendly software. The decreasing attraction of complicated hi-fi decks is another example of this trend, with compact discs a typical example of a user-friendly product which offers a clear product benefit.

The 35 mm camera is another example of a product becoming increasingly technically complicated to achieve simplicity of operation.

On the other hand, there is increasing concern over the side-effects of technology. The concern about environmental issues has escalated: the greenhouse effect, pollution, the ozone layer, acid rain. Although the level of this concern differs widely from country to country, with the highest levels being recorded in Sweden and Germany, it is now an increasingly influential factor in all European attitudes. This concern is strongest among the younger, better-educated sectors of the population and is expected to grow in the 1990s. As an example, the concern with the ozone layer has already influenced the level of usage of aerosols, with a significant group of consumers in northern Europe switching to alternatives, such as roll-on deodorants.

The implications of this environmental concern will be wide-reaching for all governments and major industries, with growing media and political pressure to be expected from an articulate, committed group. It is a constraint which has to be taken into account in aspects of new product development. An indication of its importance in the motor industry is shown in the results of the German car study carried out by the International Research Institute of Social Change (RISC). In that study, 'respect for the environment' emerged as the third most important factor in car design in the minds of consumers. In looking at this environmental trend, it is important not to regard it only from the negative side, as a constraint, but also positively as a commercial opportunity.

We have already seen some instances of the consumer being prepared to pay a premium for natural products. Look at the success of The Body Shop in Britain, selling products based only on natural ingredients, or the growth of a higher-priced natural commodity such as free-range eggs. For the pharmaceutical industry, concern with side-effects is increasingly a major constraint on new product development, while at the same time there are growing sales of natural homoeopathic medicines across Europe.

European consumers are becoming increasingly sophisticated and discriminating in their attitude to technology – on the one hand expecting more from it in consumer benefits, and on the other being less prepared to accept potential negatives to their health or to the environment.

Open citizenship

RISC carries out annual surveys in 12 European countries, North America, Brazil, Argentina, South Africa and Japan. Typically 2,000 interviews among a random sample of adults 15 years of age and over are conducted in each country. RISC has observed since 1980 a pattern of social values which is shared to a greater or lesser extent by consumers across Europe, and it is this convergence of attitudes which has made possible the success of several multinational brands. The economic integration of Europe is understood and there is an opening of minds in Europe to the value of other nations. This trend is well advanced in Italy and France, and it is growing quickly in the UK. People who share this attitude have the feeling of being able to belong to their own country and at the same time to world-wide modernity in all its various facets: pop music, ethnic foods, films, arts, and so on. People can feel closer to people in other countries who share the same interests or tastes than to fellow countrymen who do not. The need for economic efficiency reinforces the consciousness that one's country cannot develop without the outside world. So open citizenship is a key trend, and is well advanced among people who feel at ease in the new social fabric and who are pragmatic.

Closely allied to this trend is a desire for a new type of egalitarianism and collectivism, and a new desire for intervention. Adherents of the New Right talk about the need for society to be more charitable and the need to reassess citizenship. There is the fear in the radical right wing, as well as in other parties, throughout Europe that the period of selfism, a period when people were largely concerned with their own satisfactions, must give way to a concern about those in need. This is a phenomenon which is beginning to grow in Europe as well as in the United States. The years of automatic rejection of government initiatives or government legislation seem to be nearing their end. On the environmental front this is already becoming clear.

A growing number of people now believe that they should have a high degree of social choice, but that there are also many decisions and actions which can be taken in their names by government. It is fascinating how publications as different as *The Economist* and the *New Statesman* are tackling the subject of citizenship. Throughout the political spectrum there is a growing awareness that the state should be made more efficient, via competition. Individual responsibility plus collective efficiency is a model for the next twenty years. RISC's surveys show that there is a strong majority, even among the very rich, prepared to pay more in tax to alleviate poverty. Greater equality is not just an objective for socialists. It is an objective for many people across the political spectrum. It is based on the trend towards social empathy.

Adjusting to the complexity of modern life

With the increasing pace of modern life and more varied demands placed on the individual, it is necessary to develop strategies to cope with life's increasing complexities. Instead of having a firm set of rules and routines to guide their behaviour, people are developing strategies which will enable them to cope with unforeseen events. More people are enjoying the ability to handle an increasingly complex social situation. This is the generation of the Filofax and the telephone answering-machine. Compared to the 1970s people are no longer looking to make their life more simple, but rather to find strategies and products which will help them better control an increasingly full programme of activities. The British are particularly strong on this trend of the acceptance of complexity. They are, therefore, able to make important decisions on the spur of the moment and to change their plans accordingly. Computers have not only played a role in keeping track of complex business, financial and personal transactions, but have also facilitated that complexity by making it possible. This trend has affected the clothes market, with the demand for versatile, informal clothes appropriate for work and leisure.

The car has become an indispensable tool of flexibility in modern life, giving freedom to make quick decisions, to change plans and to react to problems.

We see what the Americans call a 'time shift'. People are increasingly placing a premium on their time and seek greater control over how it is used. More importantly, this time shift reflects a new determination among consumers to tailor their daily schedules to their needs, rather than having schedules imposed upon them. The demand for flexibility in opening hours is only one aspect of this.

Allied to the acceptance of complexity and uncertainty is informality. People are now much more likely to accept behaviour that a more formal society would reject – for example, untidiness in dress or unpunctuality. This informality has had a major impact on the food industry, with the breakdown of the formal meal structure. More people are taking snacks or skipping some meals altogether. It can be seen in the growth of the fast food industry. Eating in cars or in the street is much more widely accepted today. This trend towards informality in dress and behaviour will continue to be a major factor in European countries. There is no indication yet of any swing to more formal patterns of behaviour.

Figure 5.1 presents a socio-cultural map of Europe based on the annual surveys. The horizontal dimension has 'roots' on the left, and 'flexibility', the movement towards networking, away from hierarchies, on the right.

The vertical axis represents the dimension of time, with the dynamic trends, the ones which will increasingly operate in the 1990s, placed towards the top, and the 1940s and 1950s trends placed towards the bottom. Each trend on the chart is built up from a minimum of four questions which form a statistical 'factor'. The scores across the questions which make each statistical factor are added up for each individual in the sample. Each person is either at the extreme, what we call 'on-trend', the positive end of the factor, or in the middle, or at the back of each factor. Each year we measure the proportion of people who are 'on-trend'. This is an empirical way of tracking social change, tracking over time the most important changes in people's attitudes, concerns, needs, wishes, anxieties and values. RISC has developed identical ways of measuring these changes, analysing them and interpreting them for corporations in different countries.

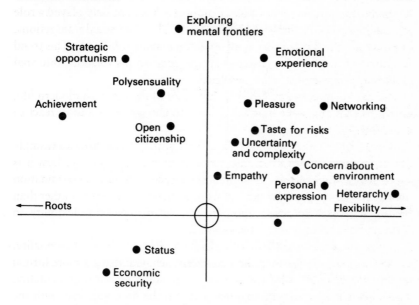

Figure 5.1   European socio-cultural map. (Source: *RSA Journal*, April 1989.)

But why are the trends positioned as they are? This is a map, like a geographical map, but shows the *correspondence* between the various trends. People who espouse similar values tend to be closer together on the map. For example, the degree of correspondence between 'emotional experience' and 'pleasure' is strong and positive. People who score high on 'pleasure' tend to score high on 'emotional experience'.

There is mobility in the populations of all countries and over time more and more people are coming to espouse the trends in the top half of the map. The examination of the two dimensions which form the basis for establishing the correspondence between various trends (see Figure 5.2) is of interest. The vertical dimension accounts for a very high proportion of variance between people in our samples. The older values of security and status are placed towards the bottom of the diagram. At the top there is evidence of the newer values in some of the more important movements over the last few years – the movement to personal drives and motives, away from the traditional values of conformity. The changes in attitudes and values represented by the trends at the top of the diagram have implications for all aspects of marketing: new product development, brand communication and positioning as well as for corporate communications.

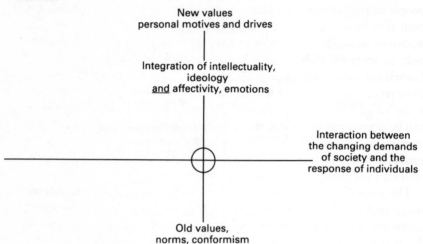

Figure 5.2   The fundamental structure of social change. (Source: *RSA Journal*, April 1989.)

The network of wider social contacts

In the past, a person's social contact was largely determined by family links and the school and work environment. These links, which had been developed over a long period of time, were normally restricted to people who met regularly within a normal social background – representing 'roots'. In the 1960s and 1970s, there emerged a trend towards increased social contact based on personal interests. With the growth of the 'small is beautiful' movement, people became increasingly involved in local government and local 'special interest' societies. Like the earlier links with family, school and work friends, these were based on establishing a long-term close relationship with a group of people.

In the 1980s there developed a new form of social contact, particularly among the younger generation, which we describe as networking. People who score high on this trend belong to a much wider group of social contacts which is regularly changing.

People join a wide range of groups in order to meet their special interests or needs. It is not expected that their membership of the group will necessarily be long-term, although they may have a very close relationship with fellow-members while they remain part of the network. These groups do not necessarily have to meet face-to-face, as one sees from the growing popularity of telephone and computer link-ups between otherwise unknown groups of people. As this trend develops, it is expected that people will get information from a much wider range of personal contacts than they have done in the past. Increasingly they will consult persons whose opinions they respect on specific subjects, although this will apply only to areas of competence where they are judged to have particular knowledge or ability. Since people draw on a wider range of personal experience in contact with others, they are likely to become more knowledgeable. Belonging to a number of specialist groups, consumers can be expected to become smarter, more sophisticated shoppers for most important consumer items. They are likely to spend more widely on products which cater to a wide range of personal interests or help to make contact with a wide circle of friends easier.

The growth in the 1980s of a very wide range of special interest magazines is an example of this trend. In France one sees the use of computer telephone bookings, with the Minitel system being used to develop an ever-widening group of contacts with people sharing similar interests. One expects to see a rapid growth of this trend into the twenty-first century, with the maturing of the first computer-literate generation.

The importance of above-the-line branded advertising for the marketing of products will give away to other forms of communication. Part of this is due to networking and word-of-mouth recommendations, but there are other reasons as well. The need to base one's image on prestige and size has lessened considerably. Fewer people are likely to identify with slogans which suggest 'largest' or 'most modern'. The large multinationals are increasingly aware of the lessening need for a homogeneous image where values are homogeneous and relatively stable. Heterogeneity is now 'in'. It is not merely possible but desirable to aim different messages at different target groups, as long as they still fit the culture of a corporation.

What is now required in place of an image policy is one based on personality and integration. Whereas the whole concept of image is exclusive and simple, the concept of personality is diverse, complex, multifaceted, changing, dependent on context.

The manufacturer should now select those aspects of its personality which it feels are most appropriate and capable of helping its integration in different environments. This concept of personality fits very well with the new fragmented media scene, but does not fit so well with the older concept of added value through homogeneous, above-the-line image advertising.

Achievement and risk-taking

There is a clear trend for those people in more interesting and demanding jobs to be working longer and longer hours compared with people in less interesting positions. Among this group the distinction between work and leisure time is becoming increasingly blurred, with the consequence that more is done outside the factory or office, in the home or in the car; and, correspondingly, there is an increased tolerance for long hours and commitment to work goals. In Europe there is a growing body of people strongly committed to achieving success. Although they have some things in common with the aspiring group in the 1950s who wanted to achieve the status symbols which they believed would give them social recognition, the achievement orientation of the 1980s and 1990s is much more pragmatic and hard-nosed. The group is far more concerned with achieving success in terms of personal satisfaction and enjoyment and much less with achieving recognition from others.

Many of these people are prepared to take significant risks to get what they want out of life. For those with a strong need for achievement, smart shopping is an imperative in order to achieve the best use of their available resources and to demonstrate their ability to be a winner. There is a tendency to identify with a major product purchase in such a way that if the product lets them down, they feel that they have not made a smart decision. They react correspondingly strongly against the product or brand.

As a result of this, the expectations for product performance and reliability of any important purchase are rising all the time. The products with a reputation for performance and reliability are increasingly attractive, even if at a premium price, as long as the price can be seen as justified in relation to the extra perceived quality. This has resulted in a general trading-up among large sections of the European population. A smart buy does not always mean Gucci or Cartier. Look at the switch away from expensive personal accessories such as watches and cigarette lighters in the direction of functional and efficient alternatives. Manufacturers are going to be faced increasingly with the need to demonstrate to consumers that their products represent a smart buy. With the long-term erosion of automatic brand loyalty, this is likely to mean that direct personal experience and word-of-mouth recommendation will play an increasingly important part in buying decisions.

Greater self-knowledge and control

People want to control their lives, they want greater choice. Clearing banks offering interest on current accounts is a response to people wanting not merely to borrow or save, but to move from one mode to the other. They want more control over their finances.

People want greater transparency in communication. Because they are better educated, because they are more aware of themselves, their needs and their rights, they can see through messages which are not congruent.

Another area in which consumers will seek greater control over their time lies in shopping. The rising frustration about time waited in checkouts and increasing dismay about service in stores will fuel home shopping. The already huge mail-order industry should experience sustained growth. The most promising area is tele-shopping. All forms of home shopping are based on implicit trust in high-quality service offered by the manufacturers, no long queues, no sales pitches and no pressures. Consumers can thus control their shopping environment.

But having greater control and self-knowledge does not mean that the consumer can visualize the new products/services he or she will want.

Strategic opportunism

The marketeer of the 1990s must be a strategic opportunist. He or she will go beyond satisfying consumer needs, at a profit. He or she will anticipate. Merely satisfying consumer needs is passive. At its best it is pursuit of marketing without power. 'The purpose of marketing now is to anticipate, persuade and influence', according to John Sculley of Pepsi Cola, an expert on leverage marketing. He argues that whole levels of executives have to be put aside in order to speed up the process of getting the best from research and development to the market.

For the market researcher, there is just not enough time to carry out the formal screening and analysis which was done in the 1960s and 1970s. A company must be prepared to take risks and push its new products. As the Japanese marketeers have already recognised, it is important to infer from consumer values and lifestyles, then produce the new products to fit those values, and follow up with research to establish how to improve or fine-tune. Paradoxically, strategic opportunism suggests both a more flexible, often speedier response at the same time as involving longer-term thinking.

Exploring mental frontiers

The final trend for discussion is the growing feeling that we do not know enough about how we think, feel and behave, and that the conventional, rational approach is not adequate in today's world. This means that increasing reliance on emotion and intuition in making decisions is considered in its own way to be just as valid as the rational and logical analysis of a problem.

There is a distinction to be made between error, exception and spotting change. Unfortunately marketeers and market researchers are trained to be analytical. They are trained to look for errors and exceptions but not to spot change. I have a mental vision of all those marketing brand and product managers with VDUs on their desks. When they see a shift in consumption on their screens, their first reaction is to say 'it's wrong'. They will readily accept a second source of data which shows no such shift. Errors or exception are easily spotted. Genuine change is not.

Intuition is most important. This leads to innovation, and the fundamental precursor, the need to spot change. Innovation will take root if its form is such that it will allow it to find the appropriate niche in a changing system. This could be from previous research breakthroughs, which must find themselves to the market-place more quickly, or it could come from spotting change in customers' needs which allow the breakthrough to be exploited. We need to know more about how to train people to spot change and we need to know more about what breeds innovation.

Where is the UK on the map?

Figure 5.3 attempts to position a selection of European countries on the socio-cultural map presented in Figure 5.1, by taking an average measure of the national population. Some European countries are moving up the map and to the left. Others are moving up and to the right. More people in France, Norway, Italy and Spain are in the top half of the map, so that the average or centre of these populations is found in the top half of the map. The UK, Germany, Sweden and Holland have many more people in the bottom half of the map, so that the centre of population is in the

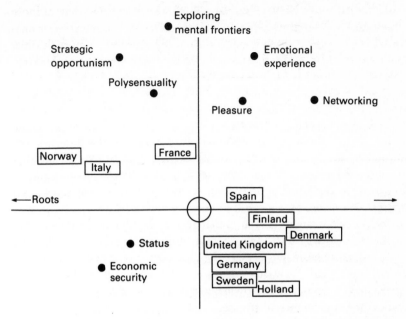

Figure 5.3   Positioning of countries. (Source: *RSA Journal*, April 1989.)

bottom half of the map. The position of the UK has changed significantly in recent years. Whereas it used to be at the very bottom, it has moved towards the centre more quickly than West Germany and Sweden.

There is still a profound scepticism among British managers about the pattern of social values which is shared to a greater or lesser extent by consumers in the European community. Yet it is the existence of this communality of social values which has made possible the success of such widely different multinational brands as Coca Cola, Ford Fiesta and Marlboro. This leads to the complex issue of global branding. While some companies have established uniform brands which command instant recognition world-wide, other companies, attempting to use the concept of globalisation, find that the global market divides into many submarkets. An understanding of social and cultural trends and their evolution helps explain why this is.

Take pasta. In every European country outside Italy people who eat pasta frequently tend to be at the forefront of social trends, but people in Italy who eat a lot of pasta are not. Therefore a successful marketing policy for pasta in Italy would have to be very different from that in other countries. The same is true of cars. Scandinavians who own a Volvo or Saab tend to be behind on social trends, but outside Scandinavia those who own Volvos and Saabs tend to be at the forefront. This strange phenomenon means that a manufacturer must sometimes use a global strategy outside the originating country. Think of the older Italian peasant in the south of Italy who is behind on social trends. Compare what is felt instinctively about his attitudes and values with those of a coalminer or shipyard worker in France or West Germany. One immediately appreciates that there is a very wide difference in these people. This is what we call a heterogeneity of attitudes.

But if one thinks of professional or business colleagues in other European countries, or even the similarity of attitudes of students throughout Europe – the way they feel, the way they behave – then one senses the attitude shift among people at the forefront of social trends. And in those countries at the forefront in the top half of Figure 5.3 one sees the convergence of trends. Therefore managers in Britain have similar values to those in Spain, Italy, France and Norway. The British marketing company must be ready to meet the challenge of the new society – the growth in trends towards pleasure, complexity, networking, open citizenship, a greater self-knowledge and control, strategic opportunism and exploring new mental frontiers.

In conclusion

- In all the developed countries, society is changing at an ever increasing rate, but amidst the turmoil and complexity, one sees a convergence of social trends which cuts across national boundaries.
- The emerging trends will have an even more profound effect as we enter the twenty-first century.
- The British marketing company must be ready to meet the challenge of the new society with its growth in the social and cultural trends of pleasure, complexity, networking, open citizenship, a concern about oneself in the total global environment, a greater self-knowledge and control, strategic opportunism and exploring new mental frontiers.

CHAPTER 6

The company and its customers

COLIN ADAMSON
Managing Director, TARP Europe

No business can create, consolidate and preserve a reputation as a 'good corporate citizen' without providing goods and services that satisfy its customers. There is little point in initiatives designed to demonstrate – like little Jack Horner – what a good boy you are, if all you can produce is a rotten plum product from your corporate pie.

Very few customers 'buy' a company – they buy individual products at various times and intervals. Yet the cumulative judgement arising from this experience, as relayed by word of mouth to friends, neighbours, business colleagues, is a very powerful ingredient in the corporate reputation. Absence of customer satisfaction means that the reputation recipe lacks flavour, substance and no one comes back for second helpings.

This chapter discusses a definition of customer satisfaction, and how a satisfaction-based strategy can be developed and implemented.

Complaints and why it pays to handle them

Achieving customer satisfaction

The formula below describes in simplified fashion how customer satisfaction is created:

Figure 6.1   Achieving customer satisfaction

TARP is an international research-based management consultancy, assisting companies to devise and implement customer satisfaction strategies.

Clearly, the most important determination of customer satisfaction is doing the job right. The goal calls for good design, engineering, manufacturing, sales, and service practices. In a complex production and distribution chain, however, where both the humans – from senior buyer to check-out assistant – and the machines must always perform competently, problems will occur, even in the best-managed companies. Such problems are costly both to the company and the customer. When they occur, practices are required to maintain customer satisfaction. (They are also required to keep the company informed as to its performance.) For a complaint handling system to be effective, it must solve the individual consumer's problem and identify and correct the root cause of the problem. If it succeeds in these, the result will be increased customer satisfaction, which translates into increased brand loyalty. Old customers continue buying, and positive word of mouth results in new customers.

We will focus first on the effective complaint handling component of the customer satisfaction equation. It explains precisely why it pays to handle customer complaints rather than dismissing them as a costly and time-consuming irritant.

Rates of complaint appear to be rising across a number of markets. This is not necessarily a sign that products are worse. They are, however, often more complex, used more, abused more. Consumers now are more aware of their rights and less content to put up with the mediocre or tatty. Even so, many of them do not complain.

Why unhappy consumers do not complain

Research identifies three principal reasons why people don't complain.

- Complaining is not worth their time and effort.
- They believe complaining will not do any good; no one wants to hear about their problems.
- They do not know how or where to complain.

Each reason indicates a loss of confidence on the part of the consumer in the company that supplied the defective product or service. If consumers lose confidence, they may not buy again.

How many unhappy customers will buy again?

Figure 6.2 holds out an interesting bonus for the effective complaint handler. The customer who has complained but who has not been satisfied is more likely to repurchase than the non-complainant, the customer who

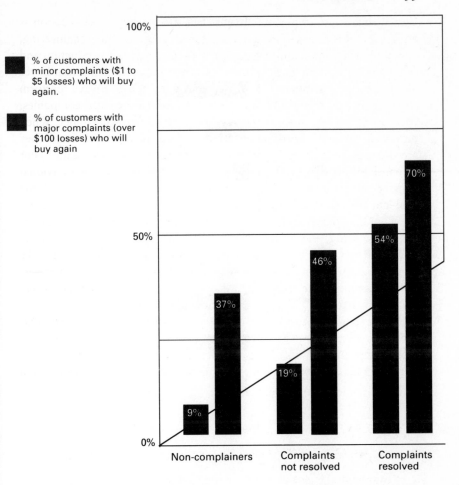

Figure 6.2 How many unhappy customers will buy again? (Source: *US National Consumer Survey.*)

had a problem but did not bring it to the company. The better the complaint is handled and the more satisfied the customer, the stronger the loyalty and repurchase intention, as shown by two examples (Figure 6.3) from the USA.

The result of the retained loyalty can be measured and calculated as a return on investment for the complaint handling department (see Figure 6.4). But it must be remembered that doing the job right first time counts for much more in the creation of reputation than even the most effective complaint handling department. Marks & Spencer's reputation, while high as a complaint handler, is founded solidly on its products.

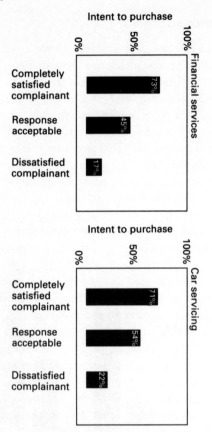

Figure 6.3   Intent to purchase among complainants.
(Source: *TARP Industry Specific Data.*)

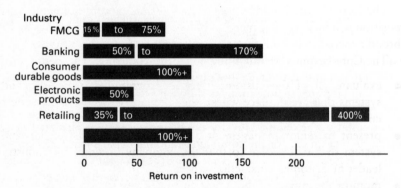

Figure 6.4   Return on investment by corporate complaint handling
units. (Source: *TARP Industry Specific Data.*)

Developing a customer satisfaction strategy

How, then, to move the company towards an environment where good service can be sustained and delivered consistently? In recent years, improving customer satisfaction has become an objective of many major corporations. Companies as diverse as General Motors, Shell, Xerox, British Airways, and the financial institutions have initiated ambitious programmes to improve customer satisfaction.

The principal lesson learned from such efforts is that there is no 'quick fix' for making a company customer-driven. Significant improvements in customer satisfaction require long-term organisational commitment. What is called for is a comprehensive strategic approach for maximising customer satisfaction/brand loyalty: a seven-step, two-year strategic process to maximise customer satisfaction through improved customer service. The catalyst for this process is the Customer Satisfaction Core Group.

The Core Group should ideally be comprised of between three and five executives from the senior middle management grade, that is, they should be at a grade high enough to have their views taken seriously but not so senior that they are unable to devote adequate time to the effort. Core Group members should be drawn from all segments of the organisation – product development, finance, marketing, and customer service, for example. Ideally, at least one of the Core Group members should have a reputation for being sceptical of the value of improving customer service. My company's experience has been that these doubting Thomases do see the light and become committed evangelists. In so doing, they give Core Group objectives and activities increased credibility in the rest of the organisation.

The Core Group should be assigned a full-time executive director. This position will be filled by a member of middle management who has had a broad experience in both the sales and service sides of the business.

The Core Group's overall mission is to:

- evaluate all of the customer service programmes, processes, and systems that are in place within the company to see how they affect customer satisfaction;
- present to senior management an overall comprehensive plan and system that will evolve so that the company becomes the industry leader in customer satisfaction; and
- monitor the impact of those new customer satisfaction policies.

Core Group members will spend some 20–30 person-days on the project during its first six months, and a further 10–15 person-days during the remaining 18 months. If successful, the Core Group should no longer be needed after two years. By that time, the new customer satisfaction initiatives should be fully tested and operating smoothly. The philosophy of being a customer-driven company should, by that point in time, be institutionalised in all parts of the company.

The Core Group process consists of seven steps:

1. Launch
2. Missionary work
3. Preliminary intelligence gathering
4. In-depth investigation
5. Quantification
6. Planning
7. Monitoring.

The first six steps should take approximately six months, the seventh taking up the remaining 18 months of the process.

The Core Group meets in plenary session and forms committees as appropriate. Where necessary, non-members of the Core Group may be co-opted and detailed for special limited assignments. It will assign most of the day-to-day staff work (for instance, much of the preliminary intelligence gathering) to the executive director. The Group takes a formal vote on all recommendations presented to senior management.

One of the most interesting analyses the Group will undertake is a review of the institutional factors that positively inhibit the company from delivering the standard of service it and its staff wish to deliver (see Table 6.1). This analysis helps get over the scepticism and inertia that often bedevil the launch of what the company may see as 'yet another working party'. The other powerful tool is to research both customers and staff to find out what both are thinking.

Finally, the Core Group must pull together its work and develop a set of realistic and highly persuasive recommendations. To persuade the modern manager, the commercial sums must add up. Here the TARP economic model, the market damage simulation model, comes into play.

The TARP economic model

TARP's market impact quantification provides managers with a tool for determining:

- how much profit is being lost annually because of customer problems;

Table 6.1 Potential institutional factors that impede doing the job right first time.

Human: operational	Human: developmental	Organisation/structure	Measurement	Systems: analytical/support	Products or services	Market initiatives	Communication: internal	Communication: external
• job descriptions • workloads • motivation • incentives • rewards • staffing • recruitment • empowerment	• training • career development • cross-streaming activities	• new positions • elimination of positions • consolidation • integration of functions • reporting structure • centralised or decentralised customer service • cross functional co-ordination/problem-solving/decision-making	• monitoring • complaint tracking • measuring customer satisfaction • performance evaluation	• technical support • technology – computer systems –telecommunications systems • database integration	• value added • range of offerings • quality assurance • standards of performance • satisfying needs and expectations	• complaint management • sales/promotional tools • management tools	• policies • procedures • feedback within the organisation • philosophy of business	• consumer education • advertising • creation of expectations • image • solicitation/awareness issues • positioning

- how much profit could be saved annually by making specific changes to current procedures;
- what priorities should be set for making changes based on projected returns on investment (ROIs) for resources expended in making those changes.

The TARP Simulation Models are used to quantify the market impact of the problems which customers experience and the way those problems are currently being handled. These models help us decide such questions as whether the current customer contact handling system is an asset or a liability.

Once the current situation is known, the second step involves recalculating the analysis to determine what profits could be saved if specific changes were made. These changes might involve such things as preventive analysis to determine the root causes of customer problems so that corrective actions can be taken to eliminate the problems; pilot testing a telephone-based customer contact-handling system instead of a letter-based one; providing customer contact handling personnel with training in how to deal with unhappy customers and how to resolve customers' problems effectively; or upgrading or installing the necessary computer support to allow customer contact handling personnel to enter information about the contact while the customer is on the phone, automatic letter writing, and so on.

The final step in the process is to balance the annual profit which can be saved against the annual cost of making the change. In this way, a manager knows whether it pays to make a change in current procedures. Further, by rank-ordering the ROIs which are calculated, the manager has information regarding changes which should be made first.

Let us consider the following example of market damage quantification for the ABC Company, a manufacturer of designer widgets. As can be seen from Table 6.2, the ABC Company is currently losing 188,004 sales annually because of the problems customers experience and the way these problems are being handled. At £20 profit per sale, this translates into £3,760,080 loss of profit annually.

The ABC Company then examines three alternative procedures. The first involves establishing a process to analyse customer contact data preventatively in order to determine the root causes of customer problems and eliminate them. Conservatively, 5 per cent of the problems customers experience would be eliminated using this strategy. The cost of the strategy is estimated to be £65,000 annually.

The second programme is to pilot test the use of a free Linkline (0800)

Table 6.2 Market impact quantification results – the ABC Company

Formula terms	Baseline	Prog. A Preventive analysis	Prog. B 0800 number	Prog. C training
Percentage experiencing problem	70%	65%	60%	70%
Percentage complaining	50%	50%	65%	50%
Complainant satisfaction	40%	40%	60%	55%
Annual lost sales	188,004	174,574	99,795	149,520
Annual sales saved		13,430	88,209	38,484
Additional annual profit*		£268,600	£1,764,180	£769,680
Annual return on investment		413%	882%	1,924%

*Assume £20 profit per sale.

telephone number to handle customer problems. Effectively promoted, this should encourage more customers to bring their problems to the company. The cost of the strategy is estimated to be £200,000 annually. Let us say complaints rise by 15 per cent. This higher volume of complaints increases the effectiveness of the preventive analysis, thereby reducing the level of problems. Customer satisfaction also rises because the direct telephone contact encourages speedier resolutions of problems which have been better diagnosed.

The final programme examined by the ABC Company involves providing customer contact handling personnel with training in how to deal with unhappy customers and how to resolve their problems. This strategy should increase the percentage of customers who are satisfied with the way the ABC Company handled their request for assistance. The annual cost of this programme is estimated to be £40,000.

As can be seen from Table 6.2, all three corrective actions will generate significant returns. However, the easiest programme to implement is training. It is also the least expensive and yields the highest ROI. That would, in all likelihood, be the manager's first step.

Thus, the market impact calculation enables a company to see where it is today and to plan for the future. It takes much of the guesswork out of determining whether a change is worthwhile and guards against resources being expanded unnecessarily to correct problems that only have a minor impact on a customer's intention to buy again.

The company that has the confidence to display and use modern methods of measurement does not deny itself discretion and the use of managerial judgement. Rather, it extends its area of manoeuvre and has to guess rather less about obvious and basic questions of customer behaviour. Being able to say why customers are dissatisfied, then develop solutions and monitor outcomes, constitutes good practice not just in complaint handling or customer service generally but also in other parts of the company such as public affairs.

The modern public affairs manager can now evaluate his or her work with a much greater degree of precision. This approach underpins the foundations of responsible corporate behaviour as well as enhancing the twin prospects of survival and success in today's competitive markets.

Checklist

Complaints:
- Are you easy to reach?
- Are customer contacts solicited?
- Do you know what current customer satisfaction levels are with your complaint handling mechanisms?
- Is your complaint department making a return on investment?

The satisfaction strategy:
- How is this new emphasis being institutionalised?
- Are senior, credible managers working together to produce a strategy?
- Are they adopting the Seven Step Strategy?
- What is stopping you from giving service?

Priorities:
- Do you know which customer problems are most affecting sales and profits?
- If you fixed them, how much would you gain?

Checklist of checklist
- How often do things go wrong?
- How often do you hear about it?
- What do you do with that information?
- What is the impact of these problems on your business?
- What sort of payback will you get from sorting the customer problems out?
- Which one should you start with?

In conclusion

- The good corporate citizen needs good products. The cumulative word-of-mouth judgement on what the company supplies will be the most significant ingredient in any public reputation.

- Customer satisfaction depends on getting it right first time; but when there is a problem, as there inevitably will be with today's complex products, it is important to respond effectively. Failure to do so risks loss of customer confidence and loyalty and reluctance to repurchase.

- Concentration on service must be more than a passing fad. A customer satisfaction strategy must be installed permanently within the company. The Customer Satisfaction Core Group, made up of senior managers, including the doubting Thomas, can collect data, proselytise, recommend and monitor initiatives.

- The choice of priorities and expectations of a return on investment can now be modelled using data both from the customer and the company to help managers develop a cost-effective set of initiatives that meet the modern customer's needs and expectations.

CHAPTER 7

The company and its employees

ADAM DUPRE

Director of MRC Business Information Group Ltd,
Chairman of the Chisholme Institute

Advances in technology mean that companies now exist where machines do practically all the routine work, and people are employed to do only those jobs which require uniquely human qualities, such as flexibility. Along with greater workforce mobility, this means that employers must be much more careful to keep and use their human resources effectively. The days of patriarchal management are over: the new paradigm for the employer–employee relationship is teamwork, where each simply has a different function within the business and where mutual respect is essential. Management now needs to develop employees to understand many aspects of the business – not just train people to do one job – and to foster a real sense of responsibility (as opposed to just loyalty) for the company of which they are part and on which they depend for their livelihood. All this involves development of the company's role in good corporate citizenship in relation to its employees.

The background

The manager or company director's position in relation to his or her staff has changed over the past twenty or so years. Many of the basic elements in the relationship remain the same, but the quality of the relationship has changed in many respects. These changes concern primarily what both sides expect of each other: the employer expects more in terms of versatility, the taking of responsibility, and effort, from employees, while staff expect more in the way of respect, communication and trust from their employer.

It would be impossible in this chapter to go into the way these changes have happened in every aspect of industry and commerce, especially for one who is writing from experience, rather than from a theoretical or academic standpoint. The writer is inevitably more aware of progress in business operating out of offices rather than workshops, and of employing professional people rather than an unskilled workforce. However, experience of talking to managers and employees in a wide variety of different industries does suggest that the quality of the manager–employee relationship has changed in more than just the service sector, and it will be found that much of what is said here is relevant across a broad section of industry.

Obviously, perhaps, changes of this type are more marked in respect of small and medium-sized companies whose natural flexibility makes them the natural place for such movements to start. This just makes this type of company clearer as a mirror reflecting the changes that are occurring across industry. It is this sector with which this chapter is most concerned, but it may be noted in passing that larger companies have certainly not escaped the effects of these changes. With the development of a global economy, such changes are spreading rapidly across industry sectors and across national boundaries.

The purpose of this chapter is to outline some of the essential factors in this shift of emphasis and to point out some of the ways in which acceptance of what seems to be happening anyway can contribute to the growth of the company, while reacting against it can lead to the opposite – loss of efficiency and lack of productivity, with all the well-known effects of this on the profit and loss account. Good business is indeed resulting from the good corporate citizenship of better mutual understanding between management and staff.

Changes in manager–staff relations

This change in the employer–employee relationship can be characterised as a move from a patriarchal conception of the role of management to a conception based more on the idea that there are different functions within a single commercial entity. Today, management does not so much 'control' the workforce in the way a general deploys his forces for battle; today it is obvious that management has one job to do, employees another – in other words each is part of a team. If this attitude can be consciously adopted by management, and encouraged and fostered among the workforce, this kind of relationship can lead to a mutual respect between the two sides. The tone of the relationship is best set by management; it is up to the employer whether it will work or not.

Some of the factors behind these changes

The trade unions have obviously played their part during the course of the twentieth century in instilling in the workforce a sense of its own value or power. However, more recent changes have had a more powerful effect in allowing the development of a new kind of employer–employee relationship. These can be traced back to two primary factors. On the one hand, they stem from a greatly increased mobility in the workforce – people are generally more able to move about between places and between jobs. On the other hand, and perhaps more important, the changes have grown out of the phenomenal advances in office technology over the past twenty or so years.

Both the self-identity of the workforce, and the responsibilities of the company director towards his or her staff, have changed in sometimes confusing ways as a result of these developments in the commercial environment.

It is worth giving some thought to the changes in industry that have precipitated the change in employer–employee relationship and which have consequently led to the need to adjust one's sense of the responsibilities of the employer towards his or her employees.

Technological change

Of the two changes mentioned above, the more startling has been in technology. There are many companies operating today which could not exist were it not for the dramatic recent changes such as in communications technology and in computers.

One example of a company which owes its existence to advances in technology is an information and analysis company based in Oxford. The company employs ten analysts, each producing two reports per day. These are detailed analyses of firms, each report individually researched and of some four or five pages in length. So far, this is nothing particularly unusual for a company active in the information sector.

However, the analysts are supported by an extensive database which is updated daily from a range of printed and other sources. The reports can be researched, written, printed and delivered to the client's desk sometimes within half a day of the order being placed.

Yet for the ten analysts there is a permanent support staff of only three people, with one part-time filing clerk. The company's activity involves a host of skills and technological back-up: research, typing, printing, librarianship, and telecommunications. It performs a support role to some of the biggest companies in the world.

That such a business can operate with such a minimal support staff ought to be surprising. It is a measure of how accustomed we have become to the apparently endless possibilities of technology that it is not surprising.

Without telephones, wordprocessors, laser printers, photocopiers, fax machines, on-line information services (and a very hard-working staff), the Oxford company's business would be practically impossible and certainly not economic. Even twenty years ago, it would have had to employ an army of typists and couriers at the very least. The company would have been labour- and space-intensive to a degree that it could not have sold its product at a price attractive to the market. So, better corporate citizenship – being, and being recognised to be, a 'good' company – is being helped forward by ever-developing technology.

Employing people for their abilities, not just to fulfil functions

The fact that such an enterprise as this is now possible is indeed impressive – there are many companies whose experience would provide as good or even better examples of the astonishing vista of possibilities increasingly being opened to the commercial world by technology.

However the bare fact of such an achievement has itself now become commonplace; there is a limit to the amazement one can continue to feel at the versatility of machines. There comes a point when it becomes necessary to look into the deeper implications of the changes, and especially into the human aspects.

What is of greater significance than the physical changes themselves is the way they throw into relief management's attitudes to employees. With machines able to perform so many of the ordinary and repetitive tasks in the office, we now employ people precisely because they are *people* and have the special range of skills that no machine can ever have. Uniquely human qualities like versatility, flexibility, responsiveness, ability to take responsibility for situations that arise, to adjust to new factors, and so on, are thrown into sharp relief by the inability of machines to fulfil these kinds of function. This is a fact of great significance. It is the central point of this chapter because it provides an important key to understanding the responsibilities of the employer in today's commercial world.

On the one hand, some traditional skills are becoming obsolete (as is most dramatically evident in the newspaper industry), but, at the same time, the commercial environment can offer more scope for personal development as fewer people are employed simply to perform repetitive tasks, and more jobs involve continual personal development.

Until this technological revolution happened, there were far fewer small companies starting up. Even in the late 1960s, the Hollywood image of the office, with rows and rows of clerks shuffling paper or typing, was still recognisably the common profile of the workplace (and, interestingly, in

Japan, the birthplace of much that has transformed the office technology of the West, it still is!).

Mrs Thatcher's encouragement of the growth of small businesses in the UK has in fact merely given official sanction to a process that was already under way, made possible (and necessary) through technological development. There must now, for example, be few offices without a personal computer fulfilling some function or other. There are few offices without a fax – the machine whose use has mushroomed only in very recent times as a vital medium of communication. Some of us cannot imagine how we survived without one in the old days, such a natural and necessary part of life has it become!

The technical revolution itself is well-documented. It is a common topic of conversation among business people, and its effect is obvious to anyone working in a modern office. However, the effect of this new situation on employer–employee relations is less often remarked!

In the present economic climate, then, we cannot simply employ people to fulfil functions that no machine has yet been developed to cover. We can no longer treat our staff like cogs in a machine, who only exist for us in so far as they fulfil a function in our business. This is not only necessitated by morality, we are actually forced into it by commercial necessity and reality.

There are two points here: technology has separated the humans from the machines, but also the more human-orientated working environment has attracted more creative types of people into commerce. This helps forward the concept of citizenship itself. People who would in the past have gone into teaching or into jobs involving more interpersonal elements than the old-style office are now coming into business. This is not just because of economic factors – such people have never been primarily motivated by money – it is more that modern business has become attractive and interesting to people who are imaginative and creative.

The result is that in order to place and retain good staff, and to get the best performance out of them, it has become not just an ethical ideal, but a commercial necessity, to treat potential and actual employees with respect as individuals. The people themselves can become better developed to their own advantage.

The sentiment that employees are tending to feel towards their company is becoming increasingly not so much loyalty as responsibility. The company in Oxford is a highly streamlined operation, but it is completely dependent on the real and willing co-operation and participation of everyone concerned. There is no room for dead wood and each person has his or her unique contribution to make.

The effects of the change in environment on the structure of small and medium-sized companies

It is well known that many major international corporations are currently cutting out many tiers of management. The concept of a long hierarchical chain of command has given way before the necessity for direct and clear lines of communication to all levels of a company. While this is in many cases dictated by economic necessity, it could not happen unless the quality of employees made it possible to allow greater responsibility to individuals at various levels.

This move has also taken effect in smaller companies in the tendency for horizontal job demarcation to become blurred. As individuals take more responsibility, it is necessary (especially in smaller companies) for most staff to be able to cover the jobs of several others, which has the beneficial effect of building up for all staff of a corporate sense of the operations and commercial position of the company. Though this is also a function of the size of the business, it does reflect a change of attitude where responsibility for the business is spread across the whole staff, though in varying degrees. The key here is corporate and individual flexibility and adaptability to the constantly changing needs of the market.

It also follows from this internal flexibility and the consequent wider sense of the operations of the business, that the staff recognise that they have a real stake in the performance of the company and that there is a direct correlation between its performance and their reward. This kind of effect has already been seen in companies which are owned by their workers, and is also evident in other concerns, particularly small ones. There is not the sense that the staff are working for a remote management and can demand more rewards irrespective of the condition of the company. It becomes obvious that all members of staff have a contribution to make towards the development of the whole company, in which they have a real stake, and also the possibility of enhancing their own position through the company.

The needs of employees – management's responsibility in the new commercial environment

The discussion so far has centred on the ways in which the business environment itself is changing and is forcing management to treat its staff more and more as human beings, rather than as one-dimensional entities existing for the convenience of the company. It is obvious that staff have more needs than just a desk or work-station and regular meals. There are other, sometimes more subtle, elements that are equally important. There has been much recent media coverage of the negative effects of 'dead space' and its negative psychological effect on productivity. Working conditions, provided they are clean, may not affect the performance of a lathe or typewriter, but they can be very influential on the performance of a person. These areas are particularly the responsibility of management.

To see one's staff as both a resource for the company and at the same time as human beings requires that they be recognised, and treated, as precisely that. This means that the whole ethos of manager–employee relations is changing at a very profound level. It is from this new attitude that will come the systems and procedures that enact a proper sense of managerial responsibility in today's workplace. While obvious in small companies, it is just as much the case in industry in companies of all sizes. Interestingly, it also applies with staff working from home out-stations (telecommuting).

In this regard, it is worth noting that there are an increasing number of training schemes available that allow for and encourage personal development. It is seen to be important to train people to be altogether more effective as human beings potentially engaged across the whole range of commercial activity, rather than to be specialised cogs in industrial machines that will eventually become obsolete. Already people are being trained to be better people, not to be adequate machines until the machine is invented to take their place.

Every company is different. What is common to all is that any change in orientation within a company in its employer–employee relationships has to be management-led or it cannot work. While responsibility has to be delegated and employees allowed to make a real contribution to the business, the co-ordinating function remains in the hands of management.

Management, in the end, is there to make money, but it does seem that the way to achieve that end is changing: mass-production has become more and more the function of the machine, while at the level of the human being, individuality and variability have become the main concerns, to be respected and encouraged by management.

Checklist

1. It is important to treat employees with respect, both as a valued resource and as people, since the modern manager uses people not so much to fulfil tasks as to handle and develop situations.
2. It is important to encourage an environment that is person-centred – decorated and arranged to suit the people working in it, not reflecting the functionality of the business.

3. It is important to develop flexibility in the workforce at an individual level – for example, encouraging training schemes aimed at all-round improved effectiveness.
4. It is important to recognise that as more creative people come into business, so they bring a sensitivity and vulnerability that will not respond to autocratic management, but requires encouragement to allow it to perform most effectively for the company.

In conclusion

- It is the responsibility of management to develop and assist in the move from the exploitational and functional attitude to employees (at best a patriarchal attitude), towards an attitude based on the paradigm of the team, where manager and workers are jointly contributing to the development of the company, the business sector, and ultimately to industry as a whole.
- Such changes are actually happening and are unavoidable. Like all changes, they will be welcomed by some and not by others. Since the observations made here apply similarly to what is happening in industry, the fact of the change has to be recognised; it is better to accept the present stage of development as a challenge and an opportunity than to seek to delay it as a threat to the status quo. Both approaches are ways of adapting to something that is actually happening, but acceptance and agreement is the policy most likely to profit from the new environment into which the business world is emerging.
- The development of people and of the company in parallel is a good example of the mutual benefit of good corporate citizenship.

CHAPTER 8

The company and its shareholders

EDGAR PALAMOUNTAIN

Chairman, The Wider Share Ownership Council

The relationship between a company and its shareholders is fundamental
to the achievement of good corporate citizenship. It is a matter to which we
cannot usefully address ourselves without first considering, however
briefly, what a company actually is. This is essentially a matter of legal
theory and history, especially history of the nineteenth century, and we are
in at least some trouble from the start.

Defining a company

In a leading case (*Re* Stanley 1906) the learned judge declared that the
word 'company' had no strictly legal meaning, and no exact definition has
been established since. For most purposes, however, a company is an
association formed to pursue certain objectives, normally of a commercial
nature; and although company law recognises several different types of
company, we shall confine ourselves for the purposes of this chapter to
what is by far the most important and familiar type, the incorporated
company registered under the Companies Acts and 'limited by shares'.
What this means is that the liability of members of the company (the
shareholders) is limited to any part of the price of their shares which has
not been 'called'; such an amount these days is normally nil, the 'partly
paid' share having become a rarity. This limited liability was certainly one
of the most momentous developments of the Victorian age; although the
principle had been established much earlier, it was the repeal of the Bubble
Act in 1825 and, far more important, the legislation of 1855/56 which
established the limited company as the dominant institution of industrial
and commercial progress.

The other essential feature of the incorporated company as developed in
the nineteenth century, and the feature particularly relevant to the purpose
of this chapter, is the freedom of such companies to be constituted as

'public' as well as 'private' – their shares could be both issued and subsequently transferred on an unrestricted basis. Although private companies – those whose shares are not freely or generally transferable – are still more numerous than public companies (and, incidentally, employ more people) public companies now conduct the great majority of industrial and commercial business and have, inevitably, far more shareholders than their private counterparts. It is to the relationship of those companies to their shareholders that we now turn.

The company is its people

It will be clear from the foregoing that we cannot be referring here to the indefinable legal entity known as a company. A relationship has, in practice, to be between people. Plato (clearly no feminist) said in a famous phrase that a state consisted of its men and, in this context, by a company we must clearly mean the people who speak and act for it. These, of course, are its managers and especially its board of directors. It is indeed these people that the layman – as opposed to the lawyer – has in mind when he thinks of a company, and this view of the matter is very much fostered by the media. In truth, however, the people who have the major claim to be considered as constituting the company are those who own it – the shareholders. It is in their hands as owners that the ultimate authority rests: the directors appoint the managers but the shareholders appoint the directors and only the shareholders can fire them. The directors are responsible to the shareholders for the management of the company and it is in this context that the position of a director has often been linked to that of a trustee.

Shareholders and the company

It is to be noted here that the development of the public company has created an undesirable conflict of interest between directors and managers, on the one hand, and shareholders, on the other. In the nineteenth century, the company was largely owned by its directors and their families, as most private companies are today. The shares of public companies, on the other hand, are now overwhelmingly in the hands of individuals who have no direct connection with the running of the business and can only exert influence on it in practice through their power to terminate the appointment of directors (usually only some of them) at the company's annual general meeting – a power likely to be exercised only in extreme circumstances.

Now the interest of the shareholders lies, very simply, in the maximisation of the company's earnings per share, which are available either to pay dividends or to increase the value of the shares. The interests of the directors and managers, on the other hand, lie obviously in the maximisation of rewards – higher salaries and pensions, better offices, bigger cars, and so on – and these conventionally depend not so much on the profitability of the company as simply upon its size. This is a potent factor in the development of takeover bids, to which we shall briefly return. What we have to notice here is that the maintenance of a good relationship between directors or managers and shareholders may on occasion present something of a challenge.

Corporate attitudes to shareholders

The free transferability of shares, on which the whole concept of the public company so largely depends, means that the constituency to which directors (unlike trustees) are responsible is a floating population. It is therefore understandable if directors do not always think of shareholders as 'partners' – the director will normally be at his desk again tomorrow morning but the shareholder may have sold his shares to a new entrant and disappeared.

The extreme position is reached when directors and managers begin to think of shareholders as a disagreeable necessity, useful only because they put up the money and requiring to be placated with annual dividends, these being kept to a minimum so as to leave as much as possible in the business for the management to handle. Such attitudes, though far less prevalent than they used to be, are still not unknown; they are sometimes illustrated by the caricature of the company which habitually holds its annual meetings in inconvenient locations at unreasonable hours – Bethnal Green at 10 a.m. on a Sunday.

Shareholder difficulties

Shareholders sometimes have more solid grounds for complaint. Less responsible managements tend to spend their money in ways which reflect their own interests and preferences rather than the welfare of their paymasters. The most conspicuous example, of course, is the massive outpouring of shareholders' funds on advertising, public relations, professional fees, and the like, which occurs in the circumstances of a takeover bid, both on the predator's and on the target company's side. That is a subject demanding much fuller treatment than this chapter can provide. But there are other, less dramatic, examples which should be noted.

The most interesting of these examples is not the salaries and 'perks' referred to above, but rather the support of activities which may have little or nothing to do with the company's business. Often these are good causes promoted by charitable institutions, and there is an influential school of thought which maintains that companies have a positive duty to support museums, libraries, art galleries, opera companies and the like and to respond to appeals from schools, universities, hospitals, old people's homes, youth clubs, animal charities, environmental agencies and good causes of all kinds.

The government, anxious to reduce its own commitments in these areas, has done much to encourage this view. Its critics, however, remind us of the fact that 'companies' in this context means simply boards of directors (see above) and it is not their money but their shareholders' which they are being encouraged to give away.

The right approach seems to be reflected in the rule imposed by the Inland Revenue: in order to qualify for treatment as a normal expense for the purpose of corporation tax, the expenditure concerned has to be justified as wholly and exclusively incurred in the promotion of the company's business. Otherwise the rules governing charitable donations apply. This is the essence of the distinction between sponsorship, on the one hand, and charitable giving, on the other. The Revenue's rule is generously interpreted, so that, for example, the support of the local hospital, boy's club or citizens' advice bureau is not likely to be queried whereas the purchase of tickets for Glyndebourne would, at least in theory, have to be justified in terms of the entertainment of overseas clients.

The responsibility of the directors

For the purposes of this chapter and its relevance to good corporate citizenship, the heart of the matter is that directors spending shareholders' money are responsible to those shareholders for the objects on which it is spent. There is no reason why a company should not support good causes unconnected with its business, provided the shareholders so wish; but the shareholders ought to have a better method of expressing their approval or disapproval than their current sole recourse of rejecting the annual report and accounts or firing the directors at the annual general meeting. Such action would indeed be tantamount to the use of a sledgehammer to crack a nut.

Shareholder representation

This brings us back to the more general question of shareholder representation. Here we must note that, although the interests of all shareholders are basically the same (maximisation of earnings per share), two distinct groups have now emerged. Right up to the Second World War, shareholders consisted very largely of private individuals, and even a generation ago more than half of the equity of all the public companies quoted on the London Stock Exchange was still in private hands. By 1988, however, that proportion had shrunk to a mere 20 per cent, and it is still falling. The other side of that coin, of course, is the apparently inexorable growth of the institutional holdings, and especially of the pension funds: the London market is in fact now dominated by a relatively small number of pension fund managers and their counterparts in the insurance companies and investment trust and unit trust organisations – the 'faceless men' of the City.

Although, as we said earlier, the dominant interest of all shareholders must be in the maximisation of earnings per share, the attitude of the two groups of shareholders to the company and its directors does appear to differ quite markedly in practice. Institutional investors hardly ever seek to influence or criticise their directors, let alone remove them; if they are dissatisfied with the performance of a company or unhappy about its prospects, they simply sell their shares and reinvest the proceeds elsewhere, a policy habitually (and understandably) justified as being in the best interests of their beneficiaries. Private investors, on the other hand, tend to hold on to their shares, remaining 'loyal' to the company through thick and thin; but at least some of them are far more disposed than the institutional shareholders to complain and criticise, as boards of directors of companies operating in South Africa are keenly aware.

Ironically, it is the institutional shareholders, the 'absentee landlords', who are by far the best placed to interest themselves in a company's affairs and influence its policies, not merely by virtue of the size of their holdings but also through the Institutional Shareholders' Committee and the investment protection committees of the various institutional groups. For the personal investors, far more numerous but holding far fewer shares, no such arrangements exist, and the directors' incentives to cultivate personal shareholders or respect their wishes is much weakened in consequence.

This brings us to the question to how the shareholders of the company and their interests are best represented. It should be noted here that there is a conceptual difficulty, in that the only permanent feature of the situation is the company itself – the other elements are floating populations of directors, managers, employees and shareholders. Be that as it may, the official answer to the question is that the shareholders are represented by the directors whom they have elected to manage the company. As has been seen, however, that does not work too well in practice because of the inherent conflict of interest; and it is partly on this account that it has become customary for the boards, at least of major companies, to include independent (non-executive) directors. All directors are in law equally responsible to the company, but it is reasonably contended that non-executive directors, being more or less free of conflicts of interest, are the natural guardians of the shareholders' rights. The problem is that here again theory is not confirmed by practice, the non-executive directors having in a number of well-publicised cases failed to prevent their executive colleagues from taking action clearly prejudicial to the interests of the company.

We are forced to conclude that under present arrangements non-executive directors simply do not have enough power, especially in the numerous cases where the chairman of the board is also the chief executive. It is at least arguable that, whether by an amendment to existing company legislation or by other means (for example, through the listing requirements of the Stock Exchange), major companies should be obliged to conform to a pattern in which non-executive directors would be able to exercise more real authority. In particular, it is suggested that the offices of chairman and chief executive should be held by different people, as they are in the United States.

This particular reform also makes good sense in the more general context of shareholder relations. The best scenario casts the chairman in the role of spokesman and presenter, the company's public face, leaving the day-to-day management of the company's affairs to the chief executive.

There is an old saying in the army that there is no such thing as a bad regiment; there are only bad officers. A good company, intent on achieving a reputation as a good corporate citizen, will have good directors, and good directors will communicate with their shareholders regularly and sympathetically and look after their interests.

In conclusion

- To be a good corporate citizen, a company must thoughtfully examine its relationships with its shareholders, both institutional and private.
- The directors of the company should carefully bear in mind their responsibility to shareholders for funds spent on 'optional' extramural activities, particularly in relation to takeover situations.

- The role of non-executive directors is increasingly important, and must not be cosmetic.
- The communications function needs high priority. It must be accurate, competent and regular.

CHAPTER 9

The company and education

TOM DODD
The Training Agency

There is a growing interest in what it is to be a 'good citizen', and a developing concern to be part of such a movement. Educationists are giving higher priority to programmes designed to encourage the development of people as good citizens. Companies naturally make a considerable contribution to corporate citizenship, but they also need to develop positive policies which emphasise and make visible their involvement in our society. Companies are part of a living community and, as such, can both feed off and contribute to its development. Many would say that these contributions are limited and that companies would do well to ensure that an appropriate balance exists.

The goals and intentions of companies and schools are different but the need for them to work together has never been greater. For example, the brief given to the 1987 National Conference of the Confederation of British Industry (CBI) was as follows:

Without an effective partnership developing between business and education, the prospects for an internationally competitive UK economy for the 21st century will become remote. The issues have to be high on the agenda both of the business community and of educationalists. We will fail if answers cannot be found and applied.

Already there exist many links between the company and the world of education at different levels and for different reasons. Recruitment and training are obvious areas of common interest, but many other links have been established and developed from individual interests and perceived responsibilities. Many of these developments are behind recent government moves to emphasise the important benefits which can accrue, to both sectors, from a closer and more structured liaison.

Companies are being locked into a variety of 'partnerships' and 'compacts', as we have witnessed from such efforts as the Training Agency's plan to set up regional Training and Enterprise Councils. The government believes that such partnerships provide impetus for growth and develops our ability to respond to challenges. Clearly the government sees the role of the company as crucial to changes in education and training, and initiatives like those from the Training Agency and the Department of Trade and Industry underline this. The government is concerned to emphasise that training and vocational education must be designed to contribute to business success and growth. Employers and individuals, on the other hand, must take greater responsibility for this training, its costs and its standards.

The major barrier to the participation of businesses in education has been the existence of two different educational cultures, one concerned with the acquisition of knowledge as an exercise in itself, the other with the use of this knowledge to solve problems and serve mankind. School teachers are only just beginning to wake up to the possibility that the traditional 'discipline' patterns and divisions of knowledge determined by the universities to cater for an academic elite rather than for the majority of their pupils who leave school directly to enter the world of work are inadequate preparation for the modern world.

That is not to say that education should exist *solely* to train workers in specific industrial or commercial skills, even though we would consider an education which does not prepare people for work as a very unbalanced activity. Companies cannot expect all educational practice to concentrate on specific employment needs, but they should be able to build on a broad and relevant experience which has laid down the foundations for further education and training. They should also be able to depend on certain transferable skills of direct use in employment.

Colleges of further education, polytechnics and other institutions of higher education are beginning to respond to these needs. They are instituting vocational programmes which are being underpinned by pre-vocational courses at secondary level. This does not mean that general educational development is jettisoned – the newer proposals endeavour to fuse the two into a broader base of vocational preparation. There is a greater emphasis on 'on the job' training, and the immediate needs of employers are being acknowledged. Considerable use is also made of the various training agencies, especially in the wider areas of management training. The Training Agency, for example (an executive agency within the Department of Employment, reporting to the Secretary of State), has been a powerful influence towards change through schemes like Open College, Flexible Learning, Enterprise, and the like.

The changing scene

Recent guidelines from the Department of Education and Science have urged teachers to plan their curricula with breadth, balance, differentiation and *relevance* in mind. However, not all initiatives emerging from that institution since then, like the framework for a national curriculum, are seen to provide appropriate support and encouragement for the earlier diktat.

The initiative to have had the most marked effect on the school curriculum was introduced into schools by way of the Manpower Services Commission (of the Department of Employment) with a brief to focus on the development of skills which would be of use in later life, especially in terms of employment. Planned work experience was a requirement for those within the scheme and the curriculum was planned to enable progression and movement into other courses to take place. Among the criteria the Technical and Vocational Education Initiative (TVEI), encouraged initiative, problem-solving abilities and personal development. It also emphasised the need for regular educational and career guidance and counselling and urged the introduction of vocational elements into the curriculum which were broadly related to employment opportunities. Pupils were encouraged to gain the maximum appropriate qualifications while at the same time working towards a more personalised record of achievement. The achievement of 'capability' was central to the scheme.

When TVEI was introduced in 1983, Dr R. G. Wallace was prompted to write in *Insight Digest*: 'The initiative is of historical significance and represents the coming together of major factors in our industrial and educational development.' He spoke of Britain being in the midst of industrial change as great as that of the early nineteenth century. The need, he said, was for industry and business to have a better-educated workforce with the ability to adapt its understanding and skills – this, he claimed, called for an uncharacteristically rapid response from education. This is probably why the Manpower Services Commission was preferred to the Department of Education and Science, because the latter had failed to introduce any significant change into the school curriculum in the preceding years.

Wallace suggested that there was now a realisation that the 11–16 curriculum for most children, and the 16–18 curriculum for the ablest students, had been dominated by the abstract and the theoretical, with an undervaluation of practical experience and useful knowledge. He said that technology in particular had not been accorded adequate status and time in the curriculum, and economic and industrial studies had not been followed at all by the majority of young people during the years of formal education. In summary, he said that both the educational service and industry appreciated that the gulf between them is incompatible with the need for young people, at some stage, to move from one to the other.

Five years later in its White Paper on *Employment for 1990s* the government specified that it wanted

to secure for *every* young person a relevant education and training, leading where appropriate to recognised vocational qualifications and to a job

and

that *education and training* must not simply be about learning specific skills for immediate tasks. It must enable all young people to acquire a broad foundation of skills, knowledge and understanding, so that they can adapt readily to new tasks and new opportunities, and so that they can progress easily to higher levels of achievement.

The White Paper goes on to specify an agenda for the future when it says:

What is needed is a development of education and training programmes for young people in such a way that they complement each other in a local community and enable young people progressively to develop their potential to the full. This will involve new partnership employers, schools and colleges, young people and their parents.

Through the Education Reform Act 1988 the government has tried to create a closer 'meshing' by creating an atmosphere in which closer co-operation and collaboration are encouraged. Several examples of industry–education collaboration can be cited:

- The creation of City Technology Colleges largely financed, governed and influenced by local industry and commerce.
- Governing bodies of schools are now to be given greater and more powerful roles in determining what goes on in schools and particularly how they spend their money. Many more governors are to be recruited locally from industry and commerce.
- Schools are allocated funds according to local formulae but they are urged to be more entrepreneurial in their approach, especially in earning and attracting resources from the local community.
- Curriculum changes are emphasising elements like work-experience placements, and project work outside school.
- The Training Agency has placed particular emphasis on the development of links between schools and industry and commerce through such initiatives as TVEI.
- The Department of Trade and Industry and the Department of Energy both have supported schemes which bring industry and education closer together (for example the Young Engineer of Britain scheme, and Teachers into Industry).

If government ministers and industrialists are investing time and other resources in creating more structured, effective and attractive links between schools and industry then they must see something in it for themselves. In most collaborative schemes objectives may be concerned with a common good but self-interest is also a strong determinant of partnership.

Action brief

This simple short note should be used to provide stimulation to those charged with the responsibility of developing a relationship with education. Copy it and distribute to relevant members of the company and use it to stimulate a discussion to determine future policy and action.

Specifically, what does the development of educational links mean to companies? How shall they interpret these objectives in terms of company strategies? The CBI recommends the following steps in the short term:

- To assign responsibility for building/improving links to a main board director.
- To develop a company-level schools links strategy, and to allocate the necessary resources to implement it.
- To arrange for senior managers to visit local secondary schools.
- To ensure that each local operation builds at least one new link.
- To nominate to the local education authority (LEA), appropriate managers as governors.
- To offer places on management development programmes to head teachers and deputies.
- To support rationalisation of national links bodies, and the formation of an independent National Schools and Business Partnership.

The CBI also lists the following steps which members should tackle within the year:

- To review local recruitment, training and compensation strategies in the light of demographic trends and likely skill shortages.
- To ensure that all young employees receive broad-based skills training.
- To decide which local employer-led organisation to support to co-ordinate local links initiatives.
- To assess annually the progress in building and strengthening local school links. This should be done by top management in view of the likely high cost of failure – shortage of skilled staff and a deterioration in unit labour costs competitiveness.

People to contact within the LEA are:

The School/Industry Liaison Officer
The Education Officer responsible for recruiting govenors
The Chief Advisor for all matters to do with teacher training

If writing, address all letters to 'The Chief Education Officer'.

People to contact within the school are:

Teacher co-ordinator for industry–education links
Work Placement Co-ordinator

If writing, address all letters to the 'Headteacher'

The lists provide a useful check even though company situations will be different. The objective is surely to form a partnership in those areas of common concern because there are those who believe that the benefits to each are immense.

Society (and therefore government) has an interest in schemes which link industry and schools. It sees the outcomes in terms of more informed, and thus better, citizens able to contribute to a stable society. Many would suggest that a more highly educated workforce will eventually contribute to a thriving economy, although the direct link between educational strategies and economic success is far from proved. Most governments would want to work towards a coherent and appropriate national education strategy and this must surely beg questions about further training and employment.

Can a company afford to stand asside? Isn't the cost of failure too great?

In conclusion

- Educationists would perhaps suggest that education receives the following from a partnership with industry:
  - A higher profile because of the wider-ranging and more relevant approach to learning.
  - A better understanding of the role of industry in the life of the country and its value to individuals and society in a democratic system.
  - Moral and material support from allies in the industrial and commercial fields which would underline the importance of the educational system at a time when many teachers feel threatened and undervalued.
  - Assistance in establishing the credibility of certain kinds of learning and especially their relevance to a career in business. Many teachers

would see this as vital to the motivation of pupils throughout their school careers.

- The company might benefit in terms of:
  - A better understanding of educational developments in a changing system.
  - Recruitment, especially in the context of the demographic projections of available young adults and consequent skill shortages.
  - Having some influence on the curriculum through which their future employees are to be educated.
  - Further opportunities for training and development at a time when systems are changing very rapidly. Training and re-training require a resource of experience, expertise and ability, and links may well assist in a better appreciation of the value of education in the management of change.
  - Responsible company image. This, of course, will vary but the general point is that most companies will want to create positive images within the area or society in which they operate to assist them to function effectively in the widest sense.

CHAPTER 10

The company and charitable giving

JANET BRADY

Managing Director, Cadogan Management Limited

Many people think of charitable giving as making a donation, writing a cheque, dropping a pound or dollar in the collecting box. They are partly right; that is a significant part of it. However, cheque-book charity, as some call it, is only the tip of the iceberg. Charitable giving is about more than just money, it is also about being a good neighbour and a responsible corporate citizen – it constitutes 'good' business. In addition, it is itself now being turned into big business, with a great deal of commercial time, energy and ideas being devoted to it.

Charity begins at home

Charitable giving by industry, often referred to these days as 'corporate responsibility', has been around for a long time. In the Victorian period, while businesses were run according to a strict Victorian code of conduct, such strictness in the profit-making world allowed industrialists and businessmen – the middle classes – to be generous or 'philanthropic' in private and public. Hence workhouses, homes for fallen women, flats for the needy, even entire villages were established and, of course, named after the person, family or company providing them. A good example of Victorian philanthropy or paternalism is the Cadbury family who created the village called Bournville. Other families, such as Rowntree, Lever, Guinness, Lewis, Peabody, Sainsbury and, more recently, Clore have also contributed enormous sums of money to the community.

At the beginning of the twentieth century mining communities might have been loath to admit the paternalism shown by some mine owners. With the evolution of the trade union movement, money from the pits was put into funds for sick and injured miners, for families affected by deaths in the pits and for rudimentary healthcare.

84

Leaping on past two world wars and their catastrophic influences on individuals, families and industries alike, little really happened in the world of corporate giving till the late 1960s and early 1970s. The view spread across the Atlantic from the USA that a healthy environment where profit is allowed to flourish contributes substantially to a healthy community. The twentieth century, and particularly the period since the 1970s, has thus seen the growth of corporate responsibility as opposed to individual philanthropy.

The oil boom in the 1970s and 1980s in the UK illustrates how an industry invested both in its future and the surrounding community. Around 1975 there were few, if any, community managers to be found. However, by 1980 when most of the major multinational oil companies had surfaced in what had become 'Oil City', still known locally as Aberdeen, local community relations and environmental projects had begun to appear under the direction of newly appointed public affairs and community managers. Later in the 1980s environmental positioning in the community had taken a clear lead even over crisis community care. Interestingly, environmental issues in the late 1980s are no longer confined to oil company territory.

Corporate responsibility

Corporate responsibility or community sponsorship has now become a powerful and growing medium in its own right. The majority of *The Times* top 100 companies in the UK are currently involved in community and/or charitable projects to some degree. Twenty years ago such involvement would have been more confined to the top 12 only.

Although genuine philanthropy is involved it must be acknowledged that for some there are additional motives. It is not simply the salving of one's conscience that motivates people, although that may play a part, it is also part of the process of promoting and softening a corporate or indeed an individual's image. To be seen as a good corporate citizen is certainly good for business.

Apart from personal gratification, there is no doubt that there are major commercial benefits to be derived from 'sponsoring' charitable and community projects. Reaching and influencing existing and potential customers is important, as is creating visibility and raising the company profile. Such activity is relatively inexpensive and companies are increasingly beginning to realise that it is very cost-effective in marketing terms – so much so that foundations and trusts have been created by multinational companies to obtain tax advantages and focus their activity in this area.

The more professional a company is in handling such activity the more the company and the community benefit from its involvement.

Charitable giving identified

So what range of charitable giving is now available to industry? What benefits can be derived from linking industry to some form of social responsibility? It is possible to identify three types of charitable giving which have appeared over time both in the UK and the USA: individual giving, corporate giving, and a new entrepreneurial form of charitable involvement based on some form of partnership.

Individual giving

As already mentioned, cash or cheque-book donations by individuals are substantial. But the British are not known for continuous giving, unlike, for example, their counterparts in the USA. In 1985, for example, $80 billion was raised in the USA for charitable causes from all sources. Of this, individuals contributed $72 billion, about $700 per family, or, on average, about 2 per cent of their annual income; corporations contributed $8 billion. However, the Give As You Earn scheme, with complementary tax support for companies, introduced in the UK in the mid-1980s, is now encouraging a more continuous flow of money from individuals to charitable projects.

What the British are particularly noted for is rallying round in a crisis. Examples of this include the Live Aid concert, the Zeebrugge, Lockerbie, Hillsborough and Piper Alpha disaster funds, and the Childline initiative. These were spontaneous reactions to disasters, often initiated by members of the general public and taken up by others able to administer and cope with the problems inherent in running any form of fundraising.

Charitable giving has been a massive business in the USA for many years and people are not shy about talking about it. The USA recognised very early on the merits of offering tax incentives in this area and this has stimulated interest in giving from individuals and companies alike. It is relatively easy to get hold of figures; for example, 20 million Americans give 5 per cent or more of their annual income to charity. In terms of time devoted to charity, Americans give an estimated 10 billion hours. In current average wage terms, this has a market value of $140 billion.

In the UK such figures are more elusive. If someone made the effort to calculate the amount of time devoted by individuals to organisations such as St John Ambulance Association, the Red Cross, Save the Children, and others, the figures would probably be equally staggering. Certainly the UK has hundreds of established charities with a regulatory environment that has stimulated the growth of such organisations over a hundred years. Yet the British people are not noted for continuous giving of charitable donations; nor are British companies.

Harold Evans, the former editor of *The Times*, has said on more than one occasion that the scale of philanthropy in the USA, as a percentage of population or gross national product, far exceeds that of any country in the world. He writes: 'Compared with Great Britain, which is typical of the European pattern, the average American gives about six times more than the average Briton.' Mr Evans did go on to say that it is not that Britain or Europe is any less sensitive to needs than America. It is simply that Americans have different giving habits. The Americans tend to give money, the British their time.

Yet most people like to give when asked; and it is even better when you can double the money with tax incentives. The Americans, of course, have a head start in this respect, although Britain has been trying to catch up of late.

More important, Americans have made the process of giving simpler. They have organised it, encouraged it, packaged it and promoted it. Giving has become big business run by professionals. In the UK this tends not to be the case. Much is left to the individual activities of charities and *ad hoc* emergency disaster funds. However, recent efforts such as Comic Relief, Telethon, and Children in Need are gaining in popularity and swelling with funds. While some companies in the UK – in the confectionery and brewing industries in particular – have a long tradition of corporate responsibility, including an interest in their employees' welfare, it is the newer American multinationals that have adopted the philosophy of corporate responsibility and turned it into an effective marketing tool.

Corporate giving

Times are changing in the UK, too. The government is actively encouraging industry to pick up arts sponsorship as state support is increasingly limited year by year. Government pressure exists for industry to support the community within which companies hire and operate. The creation of organisations such as Business in the Community with royal patronage has guaranteed a rush of 'committed' companies to fund inner-city regeneration, training and environmental improvement.

So why does any company get involved in corporate responsibility? According to James Robinson III, the Chairman and Chief Executive

Officer of American Express Company: 'We get involved in community affairs because it's part of running a sound and sensible business.' Companies depend on communities for customers, staff, suppliers and shareholders. Their activities influence communities directly and indirectly and they therefore have responsibilities to those communities. In addition, companies can benefit directly from supporting the community. This represents enlightened self-interest. According to Colin Southgate, Chairman and Chief Executive of Thorn EMI: 'No business exists in a vacuum . . . we recognise that we can contribute to the well-being and prosperity of the community at large.'

So if helping the community is good for business, it can certainly work the other way around. It therefore makes sound business sense to incorporate commercial altruism into the company's business goals world-wide.

Each year American Express, for example, commits a percentage of its profit world-wide to be set aside in the American Express Foundation for allocation throughout the world to arts, conservation, preservation and 'people projects'. Some $21 million, for example, was budgeted in 1988 for charitable projects world-wide. This is a considerable commitment to charitable causes by anyone's standard, although the dollar donation is only part of the story. Through employee activity and creativity constructed partnerships with public and private organisations these dollar contributions are leveraged to increase impact (American Express, Annual Report 1988).

There is little doubt that US corporations are active givers. But why do it? Well, let us not forget that these companies compete not only for market share, but also for image. Now whether a company is perceived as a good corporate citizen is an intangible asset; these days it is a fundamental part of a company's success and how it is valued, like goodwill and even brands, on a balance sheet.

Another force driving corporate charitable involvement is competition and peer pressure. For better or worse, companies, like people, respond when they see others doing something they are not. Nobody wants to be shamed in the good neighbour stakes.

Increasingly management and staff work together to achieve a common charitable goal because they want to do it. For example, Marks & Spencer chose to celebrate its 100th anniversary by giving £3.5 million to charities across the UK. Staff raised an extra £500,000 by their efforts and a further £300,000 was added by running charity fashion shows and by contributions from suppliers. Each store was asked to support a project of its own for the local community; the projects were those with which

Marks & Spencer's own staff could be associated and involved. The purpose of the centenary project was to strengthen the ties between individual stores and their local communities. Such a commitment by as large and well-established a company as Marks & Spencer deserves recognition. Other organisations and families such as the Sainsburys make an even more regular, substantial contribution, but choose to do it with minimum publicity.

The Per Cent Club, created by leading businessmen in the UK, has proved to be the ultimate club to be invited to join. The main membership criterion involves chief executives 'staking' a percentage of their company's pre-tax profits every year to distribute within the community. However, such an approach has been used by companies for a number of years without the Per Cent Club.

In comparison with some of the more highly visible staged events of recent years, such amounts can seem small. In this context, in the UK, the raising of money for charitable purposes has created its own mythology. Live Aid has spawned a list of imitators – Dance Aid, Sport Aid, Comic Relief. At the outset celebrities had to be coerced into taking part and making a contribution. However, it has now become fashionable to take part in such events and at Hysteria 2 (a fundraising concert for AIDS in autumn 1989) jokes ran thick and fast about such events reviving flagging careers.

Some more recent techniques for raising money have been adopted from the USA, others have been created here in the UK. For instance, Capital Radio's 'Help a London Child' campaign was a pioneer of such activity and has been running for some ten years. Telethons are a simple extension of this to the television medium. And these certainly have grown both in size and complexity year by year.

Creative links between industry and the community without doubt help both sides in more than just goodwill terms. The aim for the company is cost-effective image-building, which if carefully and sensitively handled can reap more benefit than a multi-thousand pound sports sponsorship deal with limited appeal or even a £1 million advertising campaign.

Business partnerships

The third area of charitable giving is that of the partnership. It is recognised that with state and local government funds already stretched in the local community, a more active involvement from the private sector is needed. The private sector is thus being encouraged to enlarge its role beyond *ad hoc* fundraising and corporate sponsorship to being a catalyst for the common good.

In other words, it is up to the private sector to create, initiate and to stimulate change; to create business–community partnerships that serve as social service brokers, planners and builders.

Some companies, to their credit, are already doing this. The oil companies such as Esso, BP and Shell are heavily involved in environmental and youth projects. The major banks and some building societies have been running youth training schemes for almost a decade; companies such as Grand Metropolitan and Whitbread have instituted schemes linked primarily to inner-city regeneration. The Argyll Group, of which Safeway is a part, has linked its staff, stores and management team to major charitable organisations such as the St John Ambulance Association in 1989–90.

The end result of this new approach to giving is that companies are entering a partnership with public and non-profit-making organisations to create better solutions to community problems. That has to be good for everyone.

The future

The future is an open canvas for any company or charitable organisation or trust. The competition for company funds is fierce now and will get even fiercer as the community and charity sector becomes more professional about putting its case to industry. With the secondment of skilled marketers and senior management to organisations, time given to community projects, together with all the knowledge and experience of running a business, will help hone the arguments of charities when asking for support. This, coupled with a better understanding of the needs of companies, will inevitably stimulate increased activity in this whole area.

Even if the government continues limiting funds in the community, industry does not necessarily have to spend more to fill the gap – it simply needs to spend more wisely and productively.

Yet it must be acknowledged that size is a critical factor. It is infinitely easier for a large company to be charitable or to be perceived as a 'responsible business'; the money spent can be largely written off or considered as part of the promotional budget. Small and medium-size companies definitely have to think hard before spending money on charitable events. Such contributions come straight off the bottom line, whatever size you are.

However, it has to be said that, regardless of size, many of the activities are in themselves good advertisements for the company. People hear about a good 'Open Day' in pubs, clubs and shops. They reflect well on the sponsor and, in more general terms, on the 'acceptable face' of enterprise. Even one charitable event a year can help a company's profile.

At the other end of the scale, British Steel Corporation has displayed the 'acceptable face' of enterprise in the consistent work it has done to create jobs in steel closure areas, helping to safeguard communities like Consett and Corby and paving the way for similar action by British Coal.

Faced with ever increasing numbers of appeals for cash support, companies will find they can only meet a fraction of them. This will inevitably lead to more creative thinking in the form of support, from time and people to equipment and ideas. Expansion of 'giving in kind' initiatives over limited charity budgets is a better way to build long-term relationships between industry and the community.

In conclusion

- When spending, spend wisely and productively.
- Even one charitable event a year helps the community and the company involved.
- Giving in kind is a practical alternative to money off the bottom line.
- Encourage management and staff involvement in the community.
- Community involvement helps build a better business.

CHAPTER 11

The company and sponsorship

CAROLINE KAY

Deputy Director, The Association of Business Sponsorship of the Arts (ABSA)

This chapter examines the field of sponsorship as part of a company's programme of corporate citizenship, with particular reference to arts sponsorship. This is particularly appropriate, for two reasons. First, certain other types of sponsorship (for instance, sport or pop music) are much more obviously undertaken for the specific purpose of receiving as much media coverage as possible, and are part of the 'front line' of a company's advertising campaign rather than of its programme for corporate citizenship. Second, the field of arts sponsorship has seen the most rapid and dynamic changes since the mid-1970s and can be seen as having played a part in developing the concept of corporate social action in the United Kingdom.

Corporate support

Corporate support for the arts grew jointly out of, on the one hand, the tradition of philanthropy on the part of major industrialists which flourished in particular in the late nineteenth and early twentieth century and, on the other hand, the much older tradition of patronage of the arts by the ruling classes throughout the ages.

Our current view of philanthropy has been much shaped by the American traditions in this field. Until 60 years ago, corporate giving in the USA was frowned on by the general public, while at the same time industrial tycoons and rich individuals were strongly encouraged to give generously. A number of personal industrial fortunes were used to endow major trusts or foundations for the pursuit of charitable ends, often very broadly worded and able to encompass an arts element – for instance, the Rockefeller Foundation was chartered in 1913 'to promote the well-being of mankind throughout the world', and in 1988 spent $12.4 million on the arts and humanities.

The view that individuals (and their endowments) rather than companies should be responsible for philanthropy prevailed until the Second World War. This gave rise to expectations, first, that corporations would subscribe to the war effort, and second, that once the war was over they would support welfare and the community at large. In 1951 a ruling of the New Jersey Supreme Court stated that corporations should assume the same 'modern obligations of good citizenship as humans do'. The path was clear for companies to give to causes that had nothing directly to do with their business activity.

In 1965, a report was produced by the panel of the Rockefeller Foundation entitled *The Performing Arts: Problems and Perspectives*. This inspired a lunch discussion hosted by the New York Board of Trade later that year on 'Is Culture the Business of Business?', and led to the formation of the American Business Committee for the Arts (BCA). At its inaugural meeting, David Rockefeller said: 'We, as a Committee, can contribute to bringing about in America a renaissance of beauty and creativity and greatness in culture . . . solving problems that seem at once so remote from the arts and in another so close to them.'

Meanwhile, in Britain, the influential Arts Minister, Jennie Lee, prefaced a book on industry's patronage of the arts saying: 'it would be invaluable if such support were more widespread, nationally, regionally and locally . . . such patronage will, I hope, increasingly come to be regarded as a form of enlightened self-interest'. Ten years later, as this message and the results of the BCA filtered through to British industry, the Association for Business Sponsorship of the Arts (ABSA) was formed (see Appendix V).

What is sponsorship?

ABSA defines sponsorship as a mutually beneficial commercial arrangement. The sponsor provides money (or goods or services) for an agreed return, which may, for instance, be the association of the business name and logo with an artistic event, or the provision of an opportunity for client entertainment. Sponsorship is, therefore, understood to be a conscious endeavour by a business to further its own legitimate commercial ends while at the same time benefiting the arts.

Does this mean that the concept of social responsibility has been left out and that marketplace values have superseded it? The answer is not entirely clear-cut. Most companies involved in sponsorship recognise that the activity can contribute to the quality of life within a community, whether on a local or national scale. Major companies (such as the banking sector) which produce publications describing the activity of their enterprise 'in the community' will include their arts sponsorship programmes as part of such corporate social action. However, everyday decisions on the determination of budgets, on which projects to sponsor, and by how much, will more often be taken with a view to the marketing return that a particular project can offer. For example, Citicorp/Citibank runs an arts sponsorship programme which is entirely led by corporate social responsibility motives, but a number of their sponsorships have involved placement of their logo in order that this role in society may be seen. On the other hand, Lloyds Bank's sponsorship programme places recognition of its black horse logo as a high priority, but its sponsorships (such as the Young Persons' Theatre Challenge) have a clear community value.

Why sponsor the arts?

As already mentioned, other areas of sponsorship such as sport have always been seen as a direct promotional activity; huge placards are placed on football pitches immediately behind camera sightlines, and players sport logos on their kit.

This kind of 'naked commercialism' is neither possible nor desirable with the arts; but one of the reasons why arts sponsorship has grown considerably since the early 1980s has been that the interpretation of 'enlightened self-interest' has been substantially developed during that period to include an element of marketing and public relations. The arts rarely offer possibilities in the form of direct marketing – the volume of people reached at any one time is probably too small and arts audiences are not on the whole receptive to aggressive selling. Rather, it is seen to be valuable as part of a business's overall corporate communications strategy. For instance, a company can use arts sponsorship to improve or sustain its reputation by a visible association with excellence; or it can lighten a solid image by supporting contemporary works or encouraging young talent. It may wish to influence particular individuals, whether potential clients, opinion-formers, or members of the financial community, and do so by organising events based on cultural activities to which these individuals are invited. It may need to make itself known to target audiences, in particular social groups or parts of the country, and therefore choose art forms which appeal to those groups or which appear in, or can tour to, those parts of the country. The need may be to enhance a company's standing within a particular community by being seen to play a useful social role. It may wish to use sponsorship as part of a campaign to improve name or brand awareness; or, if already a household name, it may wish to be seen to be giving back to society some of the profits it has derived from it.

Community-related sponsorships can have a beneficial effect on employee morale, especially those of events which employees can attend. The need for companies to motivate and keep staff can only increase as the population patterns change through the 1990s, and this may prove an important factor in the development of local programmes of sponsorship.

How effective is sponsorship?

One of the perceived problems with sponsorship is the measurement of its effectiveness. Arts organisations do not have the resources for, nor do the sums of money involved usually warrant, extensive market research to test the effectiveness of individual sponsorships. They are not, in any case, precise tools delivering a detailed message with instant recognition and high impact, as advertising can be. However, those few major sponsorships which have been evaluated have shown good awareness of the sponsor and positive views towards the sponsor by the visitors or audience. Media monitoring is obviously easier, but until this year – when over a decade of campaigning by ABSA for better media credits finally began to bear fruit – the media have been reluctant to credit sponsors of reviewed events (in newspapers) or broadcast events (TV and radio). In this there has been a major discrepancy between sports and arts coverage. However, in 1989 there was an improvement in this position, with *The Independent* and the *Financial Times* mentioning sponsors on, if not a regular, at least an occasional, basis; and a major breakthrough was achieved with *The Scotsman*'s coverage of the Edinburgh Festival, where the sponsors were mentioned (as a credit dropped out of the main review text) for every event where this information was known. Nevertheless, a company which enters arts sponsorship with the sole motivation of achieving media coverage is almost certain to be disappointed; businesses should not demand it nor arts organisations promise it. However, it is to be hoped that the trend is now firmly moving towards better crediting; a recent survey by the *Sunday Telegraph* of its readership came down clearly in favour of crediting, with one response stating clearly that the reader wished to know which major companies gave something back to the community.

One of the ways in which a company can overcome the media crediting problem is to commit some time and money to the marketing of a sponsorship – for instance, by taking newspaper advertisements mentioning the sponsorship on the day a production opens (this has become the practice for Royal Opera House production sponsors), by running a separate poster campaign, or by incorporating the arts sponsorship programme into the corporate advertising, as seen with British Airways' sponsorships of contemporary arts fairs.

The difficulty of evaluation needs to be recognised by a business before entering into arts sponsorship in order that a successful sponsorship is not mistakenly perceived as a failure because of, for instance, lack of media credit. Except where very large sums of money and a very high-profile event are concerned, it is also unlikely that a single one-off sponsorship will achieve as great a result as a progressive series of sponsorships which allow the contribution of the sponsor to win recognition over time.

This section has dwelt on the more negative aspects of the evaluation of sponsorship in order to point out the pitfalls for the new sponsor. It is, however, important to stress that many companies have long histories of sponsorship of the arts, with increasing commitments and ever-widening programmes. It is clear that they must be achieving their corporate aims and must believe arts sponsorship to be an effective instrument in achieving these ends. The would-be sponsor could do worse than to talk to an established sponsor to discuss these issues.

What to sponsor?

Sponsorship is no longer simply a choice between sport and the arts. The combination of cutbacks in public expenditure and the development of the ideas of corporate social action has meant that conservation, the environment, education, health care, adventure and exploration are just some of the other choices available for sponsorship. This is where the establishment of a clear set of objectives can assist the sponsorship manager in making choices. The other determining factor is money; a local arts sponsorship may often need only a few hundred pounds to work effectively, whereas a national art exhibition, and other areas of sponsorship, will involve much larger sums of money. Equally, there may be a way of combining some of these activities, for instance by an arts educational programme or a painting competition on the environment. Sometimes a company can combine a very ordinary need with a sponsorship; for example, the pharmaceutical giant Wellcome plc recently sponsored a recording by the Albion Ensemble of Mozart's 'Serenade for 13 Wind Instruments', copies of which on compact disc made a rather more imaginative than usual shareholder's gift at the company's annual general meeting.

Key questions for a business to ask here are:

- What is the budget?
- Will this particular type of sponsorship best serve the firm's interests?

- Will it reach the right audiences and create the right impression?
- Are the skills and time available to make the most of it? Alternatively, can the resources be found to employ a consultant?
- Is the sponsorship to be on a local, regional, national or international scale?

Is sponsorship only for big business?

In the mid-1970s, when the earliest ideas on arts sponsorship were taking hold, there was a view that the only people who could afford philanthropy were the large companies. ABSA was set up by companies such as the major clearing banks, oil companies such as BP, and major multinational industrials such as IBM. However, as opinion has changed towards arts sponsorship, and the reasoning behind the decision to sponsor has shifted from a grand but vague notion of philanthropy towards a more targetted view of promoting a company's image, more and more small and medium-sized companies have become involved.

One of the first examples of a small company supporting the arts was the sponsorship in 1979–83 by a London firm of surveyors and estate agents, Herring Son and Daw, of a series of concerts in houses owned by the National Trust. Emphasising the difference between large-scale philanthropy and this sponsorship, the chairman of the company said: 'as a sponsor, my firm can give much more to the arts than we could through charity alone because we try unashamedly to make an association with the arts work for us'.

Another small sponsor was Coombs and Son Bakers Ltd in Leicester. Coombs decided that its Christmas advertising budget, which had previously been spent on local newspapers, would be more effectively used in sponsoring the Leicester Haymarket Theatre's production of *Charlie and the Chocolate Factory*. Coombs is a retail baker and confectioner and this was its first sponsorship. A new cake, called the Willy Wonka cake, was sold in its shops and in the theatre bar. Coombs found that the promotional value to it was much higher than local advertising, while the theatre also benefited from the sponsorship.

This example shows the value of a little imagination in reaping maximum benefit from a small sponsorship. This is further illustrated by the sponsorship in 1982 by a local garage of an exhibition of figurative paintings by six artists from the North of England in conjunction with the Bede Gallery, Jarrow. The exhibition was held in the garage showroom where the paintings could be seen by people who might not necessarily visit art galleries. The garage bought all the paintings in advance, giving them away to customers buying a car during the exhibition. Car buyers could take the painting of their choice, with 20 being presented in this way. This shows that a small local company which has decided to sponsor is able, because of its regional roots, to see the opportunities offered by local artists more clearly than many large companies.

A further factor which might encourage small local businesses to sponsor is the fact that local press is much more generous than the national press in the crediting of sponsors. It is worth adding here that there has been a major growth in local arts festivals which may allow a company to try out arts sponsorship in a small way before committing itself to a longer-term programme.

One of the major influences in developing small- and medium-scale sponsorship in the regions of the UK has been the British government's Business Sponsorship Incentive Scheme, a matching scheme designed to encourage people to enter sponsorship for the first time or to increase their budgets. This is described in more detail below, but it is worth noting that over 70 per cent of awards are made outside London.

The tools of sponsorship

Most businesses are inundated with requests for funds from all sorts of bodies in search of charitable donations or sponsorship. The first tool in sponsorship is therefore a clear management policy and decision-making structure within a company for determining a budget and dealing with these requests. Major companies often have specific sponsorship departments; small companies will need to decide whether the key point of contact is the donations department, the advertising or public relations department, or even the chairman's office.

The second consideration, especially for the larger companies, is whether it is necessary to employ a sponsorship consultant. This is particularly useful if the company wishes an event or series of events which it is sponsoring to be managed on its behalf. Nevertheless, it is important that there is also direct contact between the recipient and the sponsor, in order to determine that each side is clear as to the other's expectations of the deal.

The third critical tool in a successful sponsorship is the letter of agreement or contract. Samples of these can be found in ABSA's *Sponsorship Manual*. It is essential, however small the sponsorship, that some form of agreement is set down on paper.

The Business Sponsorship Incentive Scheme (BSIS), mentioned above, is an important tool for the new sponsor of the arts or for the arts group attracting sponsorship from a first-timer. The scheme was started by Lord

Gowrie, then Minister for the Arts, in 1984, and is run by ABSA on behalf of the Office of Arts and Libraries. The BSIS offers government endorsement to the sponsor, and matching money to the arts group which should be used to enhance the sponsorship. It is not a top-up scheme for the arts, but an encouragement to commerce and industry. First-time sponsors are matched pound for pound (for sponsorships of at least £1000 and matched up to a limit of £25,000 and certain existing sponsors increasing their budget are matched one pound to four. The benefits to the business include, most importantly, the enhancement of the sponsorship (perhaps by extra publicity or an extra event) through the matching money, but also government endorsement which can be used for public relations purposes; this is recognised by a commemorative certificate which is presented by the Minister for the Arts.

The ABSA/*Daily Telegraph* Awards are an annual UK awards scheme for sponsors which may also be used for promotional benefit. They are best described as 'Oscars for sponsors'; merit awards in the form of an original artwork which are presented to sponsors in a number of categories such as 'best corporate programme', 'best first-time sponsor'. They are chosen by an independent panel of judges from nominations received, and presented at a ceremony in London involving luminaries from business, the arts, the media and politics. Similar awards schemes are run by ABSA in Scotland, Wales and Northern Ireland for those business communities.

Finally, the most important tool, as in any area of business, is a commitment to good communications at all stages in the development of a sponsorship policy and its execution. The few occasions where sponsorships go wrong arises more often through misunderstandings of mutual expectations or obligations due to poor communication, than through a fault in the sponsorship itself.

Sponsorship and tax

Sponsorship is a payment for a promotional service. It therefore attracts value added tax (VAT), and the arts organisation should send the sponsoring company a VAT invoice. However, unless the sponsoring company is exempt, it will be able to claim back the VAT if the expenditure has been made for business purposes.

The tax position is less clear. If the sponsorship is solely and exclusively entered into for the purposes of the trade, it is an allowable expense; but the position of 'dual purpose' sponsorships – that is, part promotion and part philanthropy – is more complex. In addition, the entertainment element of a sponsorship may not be deductible, and capital payments are usually excluded. Many arts organisations are registered charities, and many companies choose to sponsor the arts by means of covenanted payment. However, in this circumstance it should be noted that the commercial return received by a company making a covenanted payment must be seen not to be 'substantial'. In addition, the 1990 Budget announced tax deductability for charitable gifts which should make this form of giving more attractive.

It will be clear from the above that the tax position is complex and professional advice should be sought in order to maximise the advantages to the business and the arts organisations concerned.

The future of sponsorship

The growth in sponsorship seen since the early 1980s shows no sign of faltering. However, the demands being placed on businesses to sponsor are ever-increasing; almost all areas of public expenditure are expecting to see a rise in the ratio of public to other income, including sponsorship. Developments in the broadcast media have already opened up the sponsorship market there, and this can only increase with the extra channels anticipated for the early 1990s.

It is valuable at this point to return to the way in which sponsorship is related to good corporate citizenship. While much of the recent growth can be attributed to a sharpening of the marketing edge of sponsorship, the need for companies to be seen to be worthy employers and responsible members of society can only increase with the demographic changes predicted in the 1990s. In addition, the advent of the single European market after 1992 may result in a huge number of companies wishing to raise their company profile in all kinds of ways in parts of Europe where their name and style are unfamiliar. The communications mix required to do this may well include an element of arts or other sponsorship.

In conclusion

- Sponsorship is one of the ways in which a company may further its legitimate business interests – which include the standing of the company within society.
- Some forms of sponsorship are obviously very commercial; others combine an element of direct public relations objectives with an overriding philosophy of corporate social responsibility. In the words of Robert Horton, chairman of BP: 'Every company should do as much as it reasonably can to enrich the communities which it serves. This will differ from business to business, and from year to year. But companies are no more than a collection of individuals. And individuals do not live by bread alone.'

CHAPTER 12

The company and its technological environments

BRIAN LOCKE

Chartered Consulting Chemical Engineer, Member of the Club of Rome

In any company there will be a whole spectrum of attitudes to citizenship and of approaches to the question whether good environmental ethics is bad business. These will range from the pseudo-macho 'I've only got time or resources for what adds directly to this year's bottom line', through different mixtures of both real and apparent logic and disguised emotions, to, perhaps, 'it is our duty to employees, shareholders and customers to support good causes that improve our image and help our sales'. What forms of environment are involved? What are the actual and conceivable effects upon them? Are the type, size, and configuration of company relevant factors? And what are the expected (and unexpected) outcomes, now and in the future?

The companies that comprise commerce and industry must not be taken for granted. Their output is responsible for most of the advantages we enjoy over the conditions of primitive man, and they are constantly developing new products and services so that habits, fashions and society's expectations evolve in consequence. It is within this context that we can consider the environments surrounding the company and the issues of citizenship and ethics.

Industrial progress has given us such diverse innovations as cheap plastic explosives, television and convenience foods. But it is legitimate to ask who has benefited from these and to look into the ethics of their consequences. Each has good and bad consequences and external effects of which the proportion ascribed in each case will depend on who is judging. For example, television may be seen as informative and providing a degree of social cohesion, or as habit forming and a barrier to communication in the family.

There are other environments as well as the biosphere – such as markets, employees, customers, shareholders, education and charities, all considered in other chapters of this book. There are suppliers of materials, components and assemblies; providers of services such as advertising, management, public relations, finance, accounting, and the law; and development and research. There is the whole infrastructure of local, national and global societies, and particular causes such as better energy management, or support for learned professions or the sounder aspects of 'green' movements. And there are more general concerns such as surround the taking of commercial risks to benefit society by innovation or providing jobs, for instance.

The company in society

Industry and commerce are not just one joint cohesive sector of the many that constitute society. They are the sum of many different types of enterprise. In initiative-led and self-regulated societies they are clearly different from their counterparts in centrally-planned and committee-controlled economies, but basic issues are the same, while mechanisms for change differ.

Industry and commerce are not just a continuum, nor do they exist in a steady-state relationship. The very many individual organisations make progress at widely differing rates, and as a whole they are continually moving forward. And they are also a means by which nations strive against each other, and within which individuals can fight for power or satisfaction. Industry and commerce seem to possess many of the characteristics, whether good or bad, of human beings. After all, it is by human beings that they are created, are run, and are developed into the future. Their good or bad corporate citizenship and ethics derive from people. The questions are: what are the environmental effects? Who influences them? And how?

Products, services and supply beyond saturation

The purpose of industry and commerce is to produce and distribute goods and services. That by itself is good citizenship, because people buy so as to use the goods and services directly in many ways – whether from shops or as transport, or holidays, or from various professions or as communications, for instance. They also buy services indirectly via taxation, as police or defence protection, medical care, and education or in such matters as management of society by parliament and local authorities.

The extent to which industry and commerce affect and provide for people's needs varies according to country, need, and type of society. However, beyond the optimum provision to supply need, there can be problems when basic markets become saturated. Then current productive capacity can exceed that needed for mere maintenance of replacements and provision for basic product evolution. More efforts are then made to sell new output when incomes are adequate for more buying. People's wants then supplant their needs, to an extent that is beginning to be given serious consideration in some Western nations. When one considers the world as a whole, because industry is fast becoming 'globalised', then there are interesting consequences that are particularly relevant to quality of citizenship.

The growth of industrial civilisation has brought much benefit to mankind – in improved comfort, better food and health, education and means of living in societies without physical conflict. But, as the Massachusetts Institute of Technology project report to the Club of Rome, *Limits to Growth*, showed in a general way, growth cannot continue for ever. In parallel, Dr Charles Parker's book, *Innovation through Technology*, shows the need to think continually to move industry and commerce forward. Innovation is needed in order to prevent relative economic decline; and technology provides most of the basis for innovation.

Taking stock

This second half of the twentieth century could in future become known as 'the age of taking stock'. This stock-taking began at the end of the Second World War. With weapons developed capable of wiping out life on earth, the means were set in train to avoid global war. Mankind at last knows how to use these means, and must forever use them, and turn over to other purposes the surplus funds thus made available. Similarly, progress is being made over reducing the growth of pollution, in that governments and the public are now pronouncing in support of what many engineers and scientists have been working for over many decades.

But what are we actually going to do with present trends in industrialisation, so that further industrialisation can derive most benefit from the lessons already learnt? All changes take time to come into being, particularly those involving beliefs and attitudes; and incentives are needed, too. For example, the biosphere cannot support the present developed nations' standard of living throughout the whole world population. Pollution is already a problem; and, in addition, there are neither the resources nor yet adequate means of handling the resulting affluence. Further, doubts are beginning to surface as to whether further growth of solely material comforts will be good, for developed nations, without evolution in personal aims and aspects of lifestyle towards, rather than further away from, basic naturalness. The same will probably apply to developing nations, too. But one cannot easily convince someone on the edge of subsistence that affluence can bring some disadvantages. The developed nations may need to lead by example.

Industry makes goods and services cheaply. And the cheaper, the more tends to be wasted – and such waste is waste of human and environmental resources. Energy is one motive force of industrialisation (human urge and need being others). Energy is too cheap, far too much is wasted, and present-day energy economics is based on the cheapest bulk raw sources, such as oil and natural gas. Electricity is one of the most convenient, transportable, flexible forms of usable energy; but most ways of producing it other than by burning oil cannot compete in present-day economic terms, simply because the oil route is cheapest except in special cases. Much the same applies to motor transport. Oil and coal combustion and products made from them contribute much to mankind's addition of carbon dioxide to the atmosphere, and of specific pollutants, too. These contribute to the so-called 'greenhouse effect', and so also do some of the developments in agriculture. If the hoped-for new reserves of natural gas materialise they could be very useful, and care will be needed to ensure their best use for future as well as present purposes in 'taking stock': thinking for future development needs to go beyond present-day easily considered short-term technological and economics solutions. Such thinking is fundamental as regards corporate citizenship – and ethics fits nicely alongside technology and science as a component of that thinking.

Industry and commerce no longer consist of individual national components widely disseminated. In the last generation much of such activity has become 'globalised', either run by transnational companies or as world-wide markets, pricing, and supplies of raw materials and components.

Industry's citizenship and the biosphere

Here is a brief summary of ways in which the activities of industry and commerce may affect the biosphere. In the past it seemed that the biosphere was so large in relation to man's activities that there would never be an overall problem. But with increasing industrial and demographic growth and concentration, and with much improved instrumentation and analytical techniques it is now realised that the biosphere can indeed be affected – seriously already in some cases.

All around us is the atmosphere, which industry affects directly.

Industry produces specific pollutants, such as gases, dusts, and smells given off by processes, increasingly through chimneys, but often just from plant and equipment.

Then there are the products of combustion of all fuels – including the water vapour that helps form clouds and rain (and may wash out some pollutants). Water vapour is present in all combustion gas from chimney stacks, and its clouds are an obvious feature of power station cooling towers, and discharges from all processes where drying takes place. Less obvious is the carbon dioxide, of which the concentration in the atmosphere has increased by 20 per cent over the last century, and which, like water vapour is present also in chimney gases. Some 5.5 billion tonnes of carbon dioxide from fossil fuels are added to the atmosphere each year. The rate has been increasing more recently as world-wide industry develops. Coal-burning produces most carbon dioxide, followed by oil and then natural gas. Nuclear power stations produce no carbon dioxide effluent, and are responsible for less water vapour emission (from cooling towers) than fossil fuel-fired power stations (from combustion as well as from cooling towers), per unit of output.

Industry increases the temperature of the atmosphere. All human activities on earth produce warmth and this adds to the effects of the ever-present 'greenhouse effect'. (Interestingly, water vapour and carbon dioxide are exchanged from water surfaces to the atmosphere by day and back again by night; the energy quantities involved are large.) Carbon dioxide and some other gases in the earth's outer atmosphere act similarly to the glass of a greenhouse. They let in more heat from the sun during the day, than escapes to outer space at night. We should all freeze if there were no greenhouse effect, but additional quantities of carbon dioxide, methane (natural gas), and chlorofluorocarbons (CFCs) add to the effect.

Opinions differ as to the consequences, and their timing, of an increase in the greenhouse effect, because many variables need to be evaluated. What is clear, though, is that serious changes could occur to evaporation and rainfall, polar ice caps and sea levels for example, through warmer air; and that it is desirable for biosphere changes to be slow, monitorable and correctable rather than rapid as seems to be happening now, with the risk that we may not be able to control them.

The ozone layer is another upper-atmosphere phenomenon that is beneficial, but now at risk. Some of the CFCs, hitherto also regarded as positively beneficial because of their very chemical unreactivity in normal circumstances, can reach the upper atmosphere unchanged, while more reactive chemicals are destroyed or altered on the way. But CFCs (and a few others) react with the ozone that keeps out some of the harmful ultra-violet light from the sun. It is not yet known how long the 'holes' that have already been observed over the poles may take to repair themselves. So it seems sensible to reduce further emissions of CFCs until more is known. These effects are barely, but just, detectable now, though continued release of these gases may cause significant problems in subsequent decades.

The water of our rivers, lakes and seas is also affected by industry. Some pollutants are highly toxic, for example salts of lead and some other metals. Many effluents from industry and farming affect biological oxygen demand, and may cause fish to suffocate; while nutrients (such as excess nitrate fertilisers included in run-off from fields) can encourage weeds and algae to grow, with similar effects. Water temperature may be raised by warm effluents from factories, and also from power stations near sea coasts, or on rivers such as the Rhine where the limit of warming has already been reached.

The earth itself can be affected by, for example the removal of material by mining and quarrying: or the addition of material by release or dumping of wastes, whether from mining or industry or agriculture, or as town rubbish or sewage sludge or as disposal of untreated toxic materials. There can be changes to sea shores and river flows, and also sometimes resulting in alterations to run-off from land surfaces. Sometimes the porosity of sub-surface rock strata may be changed. Also water tables may become contaminated or be lowered with serious results to water supplies.

Other disturbances caused by developments in industry, housing, transport and intensive agriculture, such as noise, may also in many ways reduce beauty, naturalness and peacefulness. These may all be more insidious for being less obtrusive initially, but may develop gradually to such levels where retrenchment may be difficult or even virtually impossible.

The plight of Venice has been caused by several of these examples. Water pumped from the subsoil causes it to compact, so that foundations have sunk; nearby industry's polluting gases attack stone work; litter and liquid effluents foul the canals. If the greenhouse effect were to lead to a 1 metre rise in sea level, Venice may possibly become uninhabitable; as also may many other low-lying areas supporting hundreds of millions of people throughout the world.

The ways in which mankind's activities affect the various types of environment can nowadays be both more diverse than in previous ages, and in their effects more serious. However, interactions between the different consequences can add other problems, too, especially with the globalisation of industry. This issue of interactions has been realised and studied seriously only in the last few decades. Many of the issues have implications for industry's citizenship, and in relation to the biosphere and other technological environments.

Interactions can derive from both advantages and disadvantages of the globalisation of industry. Some of the advantages to life in general are as follows:

- Goods, communications and services become more uniformly available.
- Levels of trade may be raised.
- Material standards of living, as reflected in food, health, comfort, warmth, convenience, may be improved.
- Beneficial initiatives such as education may be aided.
- Societies and governments may be enabled to become more stable.
- Transnational industrial links may reduce the likelihood of war.

There are also disadvantages to life in general, as follows:

- Cultures may be changed or lost (as has occurred in Ladakh, Nepal, the Kalahari, and even in 'villages' in the British countryside).
- Changes may become almost irreversible (for example, population migrations towards cities, or increasing trends to excessive consumption).
- Trends may be difficult to stop or slow (for example, the overloading of road systems by the motor car that has already, exceptionally, engendered counter-action in Singapore; or population increase beneficially resulting from better health care and feeding).

With regard to the biosphere, industry and its activities, achievements and consequences can confer a number of advantages and disadvantages: Some of the advantages may have effects like the following:

- Infertile land may be made fertile; for example, land can often be restored after open-cast mining to more pleasant or more useful condition than before.
- Toxic or deficit environments may be alleviated; for example the effects of geological arsenic (such as in Styrian water supplies), or lack of diet iodine (as in parts of Switzerland in the past) or radioactive radon gas accumulations in house foundations (in granite areas) that can be overcome.
- Mankind may be able to benefit directly; for example, from fish farming in the warmth of power station cooling water (in Britain); or the use of power station waste heat for greenhouses (in Bulgaria).

Some of the disadvantages may lead to the following:

- Climatic changes, whether local or global; for example, the Kashmir mini-climate as a result of hydro-electric schemes, and pollution, or, as feared, from the destruction of the Amazonian rainforests.
- River or sea flow changes; for example, as feared from the projected Narmada Valley hydro-electric and irrigation project in India.
- Pollution of all the different types, especially as would probably happen if Antarctica were developed.
- Augmenting the 'greenhouse effect', for example of industry (carbon dioxide and water vapour) and agriculture-based gases (methane from ruminating cows, and from manure). If the world average air temperature were indeed to rise by 5°C the effects could be disastrous, causing deserts to spread and raising sea levels. Fortunately there is time to take stock, study effects and take remedial measures, but there is none to waste; and the implications need to be taken seriously and not neglected until too late.
- Impairment of the ozone layer by CFCs, methane, etc., reaching the upper atmosphere and reducing its ability to filter out ultraviolet rays from sunlight. This could lead to adverse radiation effects upon animal and plant life.
- Less obvious, and insidiously increasing are the effects of noise (and perhaps some electrical and magnetic effects). There is little justification for much of the noise generated by industry (which is actually improving in this respect) or by society (that seems to be becoming ever noisier).

Also to be considered are the effects on *animal life*, resulting from such factors as the following:

- Improved availability of foods.
- Changing or evolving breeds of farmed and wild animals.
- Threatened extinctions.
- Plagues.

We also need to bear in mind the effects on *vegetable life* resulting from such factors as the following:

- Improved availability of appropriate fertilisers, pesticides and fungicides.
- Changing patterns of agriculture and forestry.
- Voracious weeds such as bracken or water hyacinth.

Finally, we need to consider the effects on the mind, body and soul of *mankind*, both from industrialisation itself and also from the effects on the biosphere.

Improvements and optimisation

The Club of Rome's book, *Limits to Growth*, in 1968 included environmental problems as one of the outcomes of unlimited growth of population, demand, and industry. Then in 1972 it warned of a possible 'greenhouse effect', effectively for the first time since Arrhenius had predicted it a century before. In 1989 its Hanover Conference on 'Globalisation of Industry – Vision or Nightmare' recognised the importance of developing industry, especially in helping to right some of the inequalities between peoples, and at the same time it called upon the United Nations to set up an 'Environmental Security Council' with powers analogous to those of the existing UN Security Council. Industry should aim to develop itself in harmony with its natural and human environments. The Club of Rome's twenty-year-old concept of 'sustainable development' has now become widely accepted.

Industry and commerce can make available their vast resources of intellect and experience, technology, management and initiative to the benefit of the practicalities of the future of the world. In both the North and the South, industry and commerce have developed greatly (though at different rates) and changes of direction are increasingly apparent. The addition of more-conscious ethics is just one of the changes the world now needs. Lessons are being learnt all the time in the course of development; and they are worth applying on a global scale by local application.

An interesting example is the provision by BP of solar-energy-operated equipment in Africa. Solar-powered pumps, solar-powered refrigerators, and solar-powered lighting schemes are greatly helping village developments. Relatively small outlay is 'levering' considerable developments in social welfare. That is making use of an underused asset (the sun), directly.

Another example is the compensation of a deleterious atmospheric effect by a beneficial one. An 'Agroforestry and Carbon Sequestration Project' stimulated by the World Resources Institute, aims to absorb by tree growth in Guatemala as much carbon dioxide each year as is emitted by a coal-burning power station in New England.

An independent US power company, Applied Electrical Services, is financing the first carbon-fixation forestry project to offset the 15.5 million tons of carbon (as carbon dioxide) that its nearly-completed 183 MW coal-fired power plant in Uncasville, Connecticut, will emit over its 40-year life. During the 1990s some 40,000 farm families are to plant some 52 million trees, and more during the subsequent 30 years as the project activities become self-sustaining. Some 250,000 Guatemalans should benefit directly, and the project should serve as a catalyst for activities benefiting many more. And that is as well as mitigating the effect of that particular power station upon the carbon dioxide content of the atmosphere.

Some of the schemes of BP, BAT and others previously mentioned, are good examples in this context, too. The BAT case history in Appendix I shows what can be done to take good corporate citizenship beyond the immediate confines of primary production, so benefiting the local infrastructure to the mutual interacting advantage of both it and the company.

Efficiency

It is important for industry and commerce to survive so that their useful goods and services can go on benefiting their customers; for the income earned to benefit their workers; and for their financial surpluses to repay the investment of resources involved, and provide for innovation to improve and roll-over the current products and services. Especially with competition for markets they must be efficient, and increasingly so as new technology and new opportunities point the way. Life involves constant change, nothing remains the same for long, and, hopefully the changes become progress. Broadly, high overall real efficiency should equate with good corporate citizenship. Achievement of high efficiency should be an important principle in business ethics.

All this has two important consequences for the effects of industry upon the biosphere. First, pollutants and effluents have all been paid for – as raw materials, not forgetting water and combustion air; as having used part of the productive capacity of the factory concerned (use of plant, workforce time, and investment); and being not available to be sold as useful product. So effluents and pollutants have a cost, both directly and also in energy terms, and indirectly in that they have to be disposed of, requiring chimney stacks, pipelines and treatments, and other forms of transport away from a factory. This is cost to industry merely to emit the pollutant or effluent, and raises the prices of its products and services. Pollutants and effluents are in themselves direct examples of inefficiency in industry.

Second, once discharged, then the polluting effluents are a nuisance to society. It costs more to 'do something' about polluted air or water or land once they have been contaminated, than it would have done to alter the process in the factory before discharge. That cost falls upon society, in the form of indirect taxation.

Incidentally, it is no real solution to 'export' the pollution-producing process by building or financing it abroad in order to avoid legislation (and the costs, or effort for compliance) at home. Interestingly, the higher the process and production efficiency, the lower the quantities of effluents (including oxides of carbon, nitrogen and sulphur from combustion) released into the biosphere for any given output of products from a factory. It is inefficient from society's point of view to have to spread its resources mitigating the effects of polluting effluents that would have been better not discharged in the first instance.

Of course, all human activities involve some measure of pollution – even merely existing – but mitigating the effects of pollution will involve activities that frequently themselves involve a measure of further pollution. So 'the cleaner the better' is generally a good maxim, from the point of view of efficiency in society.

The technology already exists in many cases to remove from effluents the offending pollutions before discharge. Valuable metals can be recovered for reuse or for sale from electroplating effluents, instead of being discharged to kill fish in rivers; most of the sulphur in coal and oils can be retained in boiler furnaces by developing fluidised bed combustion, instead of being discharged up chimney stacks to produce acid rain; and scrap metals, glass and plastics can all be recovered or recycled for profit if done properly. There is as much technology and science basically available to reduce pollution as there was to develop the processes in factories that produce pollution. In most cases improvements can be made with very little need for new research.

Of course, all changes require incentive to conceive and to incorporate, and take time to have effect. Many such improvements can be made rapidly self-liquidating. The point is that such effort can usually be directly worthwhile – which is what industrial skills are for.

This sort of approach is really enlightened self-interest. The right sort of urge (vision, capability and determination) can make good corporate citizenship profitable. Engendering such an urge, when people in industry are already hard-pressed, however, requires a suitable approach, and that may not be easy. Another problem is the single-interest pressure group that is expert in galvanising the emotions of the public, but frequently antagonistic to the very people in industry who would be better encouraged than attacked. The pressure groups can certainly contain the genuine and scientifically enlightened concern that is exploited, but the scientific sincerity can easily become submerged or overtaken as a result of public relations skill recruiting unenlightened or even biased emotional passions. Then there is risk of the wrong targets being chosen for attack. It is frequently the most benign and forward-looking whose efforts are the easiest to disparage. Unfortunately the public rarely appreciates that change does take time, and that pillorying industry may merely delay or even negate the efforts of those who have been working to the same (but more enlightened) ends for years. Accusing industry of causing acid rain, for example, and demanding action overnight, when the cause of the leaf damage assumed to be the evidence, turns out to be heavier-than-usual infestation of the leaf-miner insect pest (a recent example) damages the cause of sensible progress towards reduction of atmospheric pollution generally. Sadly, there are many examples of such easily-won meretricious publicity becoming inimical to real improvement.

However, there is much real progress in these fields continually being made by industry, often in conjunction with government (actively aided by people from industry), with the British Standards Institution (with representatives of professional and industrial bodies), and with universities and research institutions (that usually have industrial people on guiding committees). This contributes to good corporate citizenship. Perhaps companies should make more of such activities in their annual reports. Britain has been leading the way with pollution reduction for over a hundred years, and could more actively develop its export markets in both technology and plant.

Safety

Improving safety is another form of good corporate citizenship. True, some serious disasters such as Bhopal, or Flixborough or Seveso or Chernobyl have seemingly resulted from stupidity. Others, such as flight KAL 007 or the *Herald of Free Enterprise*, or the King's Cross fire, seem to have been disasters just waiting to happen. These all show that we must never be complacent or arrogant on the subject of safety. To those who suffer in whichever way, there is no excuse – but it is no solution to condemn industry for its mere existence or to blame its motives by distorting them. As well as general good management, there is a valuable specific way ahead, known as quality assurance (QA) (see Appendix III). This is a complete philosophy engendered by the British Standards Institution in the form of British Standard 5750 and its associated buttressing Standards. This covers many of the bases for improving safety.

The QA approach can help reduce the numbers of malformed small production components; or improve the overall design, procurement and construction of a chemical or any other factory; or raise the level of health care in a community or of service in a hospital, for example. This whole concept of raising the level of service is gaining ground in many directions far wider now than the engineering industry in which it all began. QA is an approach that can be applied not only to all corporate activity both inside and outside industry, but also within society so as to raise society's levels of service to its citizens.

Safety is a special component of QA, and has its own specialist approaches. Hazard analysis (HAZAN) and hazard and operability analysis (HAZOP) are established practices in industry, particularly (but not exclusively) in the chemical and petroleum industries. There are many professional and industrial organisations involved in obviating the causes and bases of industrial accidents and disasters. Some of those in the lead are the Institution of Chemical Engineers, the Health and Safety Executive (Department of the Environment), the Safety and Reliability Directorate (UKAEA), the Safety and Reliability Society and the Insurance Technical Bureau. Adopting, and developing these types of approach world-wide would indeed improve corporate citizenship in most walks of life.

There are several interesting initiatives that represent enlightened, indeed charitable, good citizenship. One is the 'Register of Engineers for Disaster Relief' centred on the Institution of Civil Engineers. Selected volunteers with the right sort of experience in any engineering discipline can be sent rapidly where their expertise is urgently needed. The Royal Society maintains a register of specialists in volcanic emergencies.

A rather special concern arose from the 1986 disaster at Chernobyl that put 300 people into hospital with serious radiation doses, and of which 31 died. This led Sir Frederick Warner to set up a nucleus of 100 volunteers from the top UK scientists and engineers over 65 years old, prepared to carry out initial surveys of comparable events and accept a radiation dose about a quarter of the standard accepted as lethal. The list is of selected specialists of great expertise beyond the age where radiation exposure could be serious for younger engineers. It is potentially available to sponsors.

Of special interest, too, is the Watt Committee on Energy, because most aspects of fire, explosion, power station pollution, and nuclear issues and accidents, for example, have energy implications. This top-level independent charitable body representing 63 professional organisations, exists to outline energy issues of consequence to the public at large. It has published studies on many matters of public concern such as the Chernobyl accident, and acid rain, and is currently engaged on an umberella exercise on the greenhouse effect, and on a number of other energy-related topics of public interest.

Despite the appalling examples given earlier, and the disasters that will presumably, and sadly, always happen, nevertheless safety standards are continually being raised. The improvements over the last generation have been marked. Accidents are caused not by technology, but by the lack of proper application of it.

Risk

Safety can never be 100 per cent guaranteed, of course, but continuing effort can help save people from the worst consequences of their own failings. After all, technology does not cause troubles; it is necessarily mankind's misuse of it, or negligence, that is always at fault. Risk is not, it seems, properly understood by most people, nor even by much of top management of industry, commerce, Whitehall or Westminster.

Very briefly, in the UK the risk to an individual of death in any one year from being hit by a meteorite, would be 1 in 100 billion; or by lightning, 1 in 10 million. The risk per year from drowning, domestic gas explosion, being hit by a falling object, excessive cold, electrocution, poisonous gas and vapours, accident on a railway or by air travel, would each be 1 in 1 million. From accident caused by fire, or at work, or by homicide the figure is 1 in 100,000; and by suicide or self-inflicted injury, road accident or accident at home, the risk of death each year is about 1 in 10,000.

Occupational risks of fatal accidents are expressed as the fatal accident rate (FAR) – the number of fatal accidents expected per 100 million exposed hours, and roughly corresponds to the number of deaths per 1,000 workers. The FAR for simply staying at home is 3; that from agricultural work is 10; that from air travel, 240; and that from riding a motorcycle, 1,000 (these statistics are from *The Health and Safety Factbook*, Professional Publishing Ltd, 1989). Despite much progress the reduction of these figures is clearly a target for all industry.

Understanding risk involves numeracy in education as well as literacy, and present developments in education are encouraging. Technology is now one of the curriculum foundation subjects that encourages numeracy, and several organisations, such as DESTECH (see Appendix V), have been encouraging its development over many years. Young people's enthusiasm for technology, and interest and capability in it, can be engendered to the benefit of society as a whole and of general understanding of industry and its management.

Another valuable approach is the initiative of some countries in providing tax incentives for 'mature' education. Not only do such measures simplify impending early retirement problems, they help to improve understanding of up-to-date issues and dissolve away uninformed prejudicies.

Improved communications reciprocally between society and commerce and industry will be a valuable component of good corporate citizenship.

Freedom from trouble

Another important aspect of good corporate citizenship is the supply of goods and services that are fit for their purposes, and are free from trouble. People must not expect conditions to remain static, and must accept that life continually moves ahead accommodating the progress that results from initiative. As consumers, people pay for progress because they like the improvements. Freedom from trouble is one of these. Motor cars, home heating, foreign holidays and cheap fashion clothing for instance, are basically far more reliable than a generation ago.

But numbers increase, and concentration and congestion cause problems. Motorway hold-ups, air-travel delays, train crowding, and shop check-out queues are just some examples of the need for further good corporate citizenship beyond merely making available the products and services of industry. High load factor that is good for short-term apparent profitability can be so high as to be inimical to overall convenience, because slight overload then has a disproportionate effect on comfort and peace of mind.

The consumer surely has every right to expect that mass services advertised are reliably delivered, especially those lauded in polished television advertising. Post, railway, telephone and investment services, for example, could perhaps all benefit by companies contributing to collective corporate citizenship by improving the probability of advertised benefits actually meeting their own advertised criteria.

A similar problem arises with mass-market domestic fast-food supplies. Breadth of choice is generally wide and little affected by seasons; and convenience in preparation and cooking are also far greater than even a generation ago. But companies need continually to watch out for the complications that so often follow soon after developments in production, packaging and distribution for larger quantities and speedier delivery. These can include unforseen infection build-ups (for example, salmonella or listeria) or insane blackmail (for example, food contamination by pressure groups).

Here again the BS 5750 QA principles can stand all developments and improvements in good stead – provided, that is, the standard is used as a stimulus to new thought, and not just as a checklist on past practices. Quality, service, and real efficiency derive from a state of mind continually to perform as well as possible. Cheapness by itself, and myopic commercial 'economy', are of little long-term benefit to a company if it mortgages its future goodwill and business for short-term profit. Real efficiency is entirely different from the non-technologist's idea of economy or profitability.

Reduction of trouble is one of the purposes of innovation, and of research and development. Two opposite types of example form an interesting contrast in the results of official thinking, or lack of thinking, about good citizenship. British Rail is having trouble with overcrowding on many routes and seems to be taking a long time to deal with its problems. Yet its provision of wheelchair access, and its measures for helping disabled people to use trains and stations are in fact helping the overcrowding problems. Not only are the disabled helped directly; they then cause fewer hold-ups for other people and ease the flow of passengers generally.

By contrast, with all the desirable renewing of telephone and power cables, and gas and water mains, pavements and roads are being dug up. Disturbances to roads and footpaths indirectly mitigate some of the direct benefits of the improved services. Similarly, building developments may be fine, but the removal and non-replacement of street name boards, coupled with the inconsistencies between direction signs and road maps and street plans makes navigation more difficult for strangers despite improvements in motorways and trunk roads. There are examples all around, of opportunities to improve corporate citizenship.

Development, research and innovation

Research and development are usually, wrongly, considered in that order, and are frequently confused in the same way as are science and engineering. Engineering is building the practical bases of industrial progress that benefits society. It uses such science as may be available along with judgement in using people and materials to make things, and of what the market may need, and of all the many aspects of getting the job done – from design (of structure, process, function and purpose), to styling and fashion, including costs, planning, production and the input to marketing. Engineering something quite new usually requires development, which is finding out those things one knows one does not know, and being prepared for unforeseen pitfalls of the previously unknowable, or unguessable. It may be necessary to set going some applied research (often of high order) to provide extra science to assist development. And some pure research already done elsewhere may be adaptable for the purpose in hand.

Innovation is not invention, but is achieved when an invention has been successfully developed and firmly established on the market. Many innovations, such as the zip fastener, sticky tape, and glass-fibre boats, for example, took decades before the needed lessons had been discovered and fully learnt, with their applications and markets fully and reliably established.

Innovation, with its chain of antecedents, is a good example of initiative becoming good corporate citizenship – when successful. Unsuccessful inventors whose efforts do not become innovations, sadly, waste resources as well, eventually, as their own confidence.

The point is that striving for progress requires urge. Good citizenship always was a burden because it required people to think and act beyond the immediate short-term obvious purpose. Provision has to be made somewhere for the resources needed for progress, and they can only come from the surpluses that commerce and industry make on their run-of-the-mill activities. The commercial and industrial infrastructures, too, are important for innovation. That is why countries such as Japan and Korea, good in vertical integration for specific product lines, are trying to establish the sorts of infrastructure that we in Britain have become so used to for so long that we may forget its very importance.

Commerce and industry will presumably go on evolving, reflecting the ever-increasing developments of technology. More and better goods require ever-fewer workpeople in factories; services are continually increasing, being themselves overtaken by growth in information handling. So companies can become ever closer to, and interlinked with, the different types of society of which they are part. All this contributes to good corporate citizenship.

In conclusion

- A company interacts with its different environments whether it likes it or not.
- Deleterious effects on the environment, of whatever type, will 'kick back' in the end, and will cost money.
- Effects caused by use of technology can be good or bad or a mixture of both. The bad ones can also be overcome by the proper use of technology.
- Standards expected of industry seem to be advancing all the time. Firms in the lead as regards such standards can become the new market leaders, leaving the others having to catch up, usually at greater cost.
- An environmentally sensible factory or company is more profitable overall than an environmentally insensitive one.

- Factory and company managers, workers, customers and legislators are all human beings. The way they collectively run their interlinked affairs is up to them. It is they, collectively, who develop good corporate citizenship.
- To get things done requires leadership with urge – vision, capability and determination – not, by any means, the loudest voice.
- There are no 'quick fixes' to good corporate citizenship. It comes from linked individual and collective responsibility.
- Corporate citizenship involves everyone – in companies, professions, trade unions, and local, national and international governments – living and working together as individuals.

PART III

Managing the corporate communications function – priority sectors

CHAPTER 13

Making the most of the company case and getting the message across

Coming to grips with a subject as large as good corporate citizenship is not easy. Thus far in this book the scene has been set, and special areas of importance have been identified and relevant priorities reviewed. This chapter attempts to pull the threads together so that the reader can determine the necessary action to be taken. First, though, we must identify the key criteria.

Key criteria involve the recognition of what the company has to offer to all its target audiences. Welding the various aspects of its contribution together establishes the company as a corporate citizen. Adding emphasis to this total concept, to 'polish' the reputation of the company, to enhance it and to promulgate the company's record of achievement, enables the company to be seen as a 'good' company – a good corporate citizen.

To enable this to be done, the facts, as they exist, should be examined. The point to note here is a strange one – *the facts are not always the facts*. The point was made in a Granada Lecture at the Guildhall in London some years ago by Lord Jenkins (then Roy Jenkins) in his capacity as Home Secretary. He was referring to the facts as recognised by him and based on reference data and relevant statistics, and he indicated that these often did not exist by comparison with issues and facts as perceived by the general public as a result of reading the morning newspaper or watching the television news. As a result key issues which needed to be dealt with urgently had to wait until the issues raised in the public perception had been dealt with. The facts as perceived by the people were often very different from the facts as perceived by the 'experts'. It is an important lesson.

So what facts should be considered?

Information is power

This simple fact is only now achieving recognition in the boardroom. In tomorrow's business era the director who ignores this basic truth does so at his or her peril. But information and its effective management is not a simple subject. It is many-faceted. So what does it comprise? And how should the function be managed to ensure that the company makes the most of its case and gets credit when and where this is due? It is important to look at the overall issues and signpost for the company and the reader, the different areas involved and how they interface with each other to form the composite whole, the corporate reputation of the company.

The company communicates – all the time

The first point to recognise is that the company is communicating – all the time. Every second of every day thousands of different messages are being transmitted to different target groups. So the who and the what should be identified.

Who is doing the communicating? Just about everyone in the company, from the receptionist to the factory worker, to the Board member. Also, messages are being transmitted through large numbers of people associated with the company, from the families of employees to suppliers; from local community officials to those working for firms servicing the company's specialist needs.

What is being communicated: various messages through formal routes, where considered messages are targeted from using display advertising, to letters to customers, in promotion material prepared and distributed by the company (the product or service brochures and similar items) to the notices which the company displays on the staff notice boards, from the company logo and corporate identity to the Annual Report and Accounts. Informal information about the company, too, is being communicated all the time: it is being passed at informal management and staff briefings, in the gossip columns of the staff newspaper and in myriad other ways right down to the information exchanged between small groups of employees at the local pub. Also of course, media comment forms an important element of the communications mix.

In some areas the messages are carefully thought through and targeted – in others the process can be dangerously haphazard, to say the least! As an example, just consider the formalities involved in preparing and presenting the Annual Report and Accounts. The Board and its auditors consider carefully just about every nuance in every sentence of the chairman's statement. The auditors work to the high standards of their Institute of Chartered Accountants and question any 'grey' areas before they sign off the accounts. By contrast, the simpler, more attractive and generally illustrated 'short version' of the Annual Report which is prepared and distributed to employees and/or shareholders (and which can be more widely read), does not have to be formally and externally signed off or 'authorised' by anyone at all. As a result, the incompetent or devious or dishonest manager or director can 'massage' or 'manage' the information it contains to give an entirely different, even false or misleading picture, using basically the same information but perhaps not quite all of it! General information added or subtracted – and even illustrations – can be used to achieve a different 'gloss'. This, in turn, can lead the reader to reach an entirely different set of conclusions!

And again, does the company make the most of that key document, the formal Annual Report and Accounts? Very rarely does it contain information which can help the reader form a fully rounded view of the company. Both Board and auditors would seem committed to delivering the minimum standards of information they can get away with. Only rarely does the company management recognise the added-value in presenting an attractive, illustrated and 'rounded' picture of the company as a whole. What a pity!

But things are changing. Many companies are now adding information on other areas key to their successful future business, like information on the work of the company in the local community, and in research and development; or information about the company's contributions (in cash or secondment) to charity, to the arts, to sports or other sponsorship. Much are such moves to be welcomed. But it is still, alas, a case of little and late . . .

The company as a good corporate citizen recognises the need for an even two-way flow of information and a relationship of equals between the company and those represented by all its key target groups – from employees to the company's owners, the shareholders.

The importance of consistency in communications

We have recognised the nature and number of messages emanating from the company. We must also agree the importance of their consistency. It is potentially damaging, and also highly wasteful for the messages to fight each other and for one to cancel the other out. For example, the company may be following a policy of wage restraint. As a result, the Personnel Director may be briefing the unions and the work force on the reasons for this. Perhaps it is because the company intends to embark on a major capital investment programme. At the other end of the scale, the Board may have decided to make an acquisition and needs the Managing

Director to inform key groups in the city, including the interested brokers, specialist analysts, appropriate business and trade media, perhaps even the shareholders, of the facts related to the company's excellent profit record over past years. Depending on how sensitively and imaginatively both operations are handled, the company may enjoy a smooth ride or suffer an extremely bumpy one! The results could affect many things, including the share price, which could move up or down significantly!

It all starts with research

There are many, many books devoted to the importance of market and other research in business. Suffice here to say that if the company is not confident that it is well equipped with background research material in the relevant areas then it should take the immediate decision to acquire this information. To try to operate a successful business without it is rather like trying to make bricks without straw!

What can market research tell you?

- The actual size of the market, both for home sales and for export.
- The potential size of the market, for existing and for new products.
- The potential size of the market, given certain conditions such as a new product launch, a new programme of marketing and corporate communication, both by the company and by competitors.
- The company's probable sales over a period, given a certain level of expenditure on corporate communications and promotion generally.

Research can also help the company develop a profile of actual and potential customers, by income, socio-economic group and location, if the company is engaged in selling consumer products. However, if the company is concerned with marketing industrial products or services, research can be used to produce a detailed picture of customers, what kinds of organisation are involved, and the identity of the decision-makers in those organisations. Needs and attitudes can also be determined by research, and it can be of superlative use in the diagnosis of problems which may be facing the company or which are lurking in the background waiting to be identified as problems of the future.

There are, of course, many different techniques used in relation to the provision of research services. In brief, these include: desk research; face-to-face interviewing; telephone interviewing; omnibus surveys; group discussions, and hall tests and clinics. In addition, it is important to consider the advantages of commissioning regular tracking surveys on company image so that the company can recognise what levels of progress are being achieved – in general terms, and also in specific terms – against identified competitors.

Corporate identity and why it is important

It has been said earlier in this book that the company has a living personality, and that this can be personalised, in research, as male or female, young or old, working, middle or 'yuppy' class. The company's corporate identity is critical, it is the visible 'face' of the company. If it is good and works well, is co-ordinated effectively and promoted efficiently, it can work hard for the company and is a most valuable asset. If not, the company could be losing out more than it can conceivably imagine.

Naturally enough, there is a corporate identity 'industry' milking this lucrative market. To most industrialists it may sound like the story of 'The Emperor's New Clothes' – the benefits seem invisible against the costs which often appear exorbitant. To hold this view without having taken the trouble to study the area is dangerously simplistic and could damage the company's interests. Again, to consider automatically that only the biggest can be considered because only they can produce the best results for the company is equally short-sighted. It is the nature of creative services that the original mind sometimes finds it hard to develop and work imaginatively in the corporate culture of a large organisation. So, in the case of shopping for a new or updated identity, small may prove to be very beautiful indeed!

How is corporate identity developed? In a word, it must be able to identify the company and transmit a message or 'general feel' for the company personality in just about every possible way. It is generally expressed as a company logo with or without the company name. This is interpreted in many ways, including:

- On the company letterhead, other stationery and in print work generally.
- On the packaging of the company's products or services.
- In display and other advertising.
- On the face of the company buildings and within them – in relevant signposting.
- On staff uniforms when worn.
- On the company's transport fleet of vans, etc.
- In sponsorship and other corporate activities.

A further point to remember is that the corporate identity evolves all the time and, therefore, the matter should be kept under constant review.

Changes should generally be made slowly and subtly. The matter of the introduction of a completely new corporate identity needs thorough and most thoughtful consideration and is a matter for agreement with the Board of directors.

It follows that the introduction of a new or updated corporate identity to all the company's key target groups is a matter for much serious reflection and planning.

Managing the communications function

To get the company's message across it is, of course, critical that the communications function must march in step with the company's corporate objectives and strategy. A separate and distinct set of communications objectives should be set together with the relevant strategy. These should be agreed at Board level and put in the charge of a senior executive in the company, preferably a Board director.

The overall reputation of the company relates closely to the operation and effectiveness of its corporate communications programme. Communications outside the company, in turn, break down into several distinct areas: public relations (to include exhibitions and trade fairs); media relations; crisis management; government relations; community relations; corporate identity; corporate advertising; and market support (to include advertising and sales promotion).

Media relations

Companies, and executives within those companies, seem to take diametrically opposite attitudes to media relations. Probably all would agree that media play a critical role. Some consider it is important to understand how the media work, that they are an inexpensive management tool to be used effectively, on which time and care should be spent. Others, sometimes quite vehemently, see the media as 'the enemy', the opposition, to be avoided where possible. Most treat journalists warily, sometimes with what amounts to extreme cynicism.

The interdependence of the company and media

In relation to the media there is one simple fact which the reader of this book should recognise and accept. The relationship of the company with media is not one of 'them' and 'us'. The company and media are interdependent. So the company is stuck with the media and the media are stuck with the company. It behoves the enlightened director to make the best of the position. And the best can be very, very good indeed.

The company taking the trouble to understand the different priorities of the differing types of media, from trade and business, to local, regional and national; from press to broadcasting, really has to hand an invaluable tool which can be used quickly, is flexible and can work extremely well in the company's interests ... Effective media relations can certainly help to get the company message across.

It is most important for the company, and any one within it, not to attempt to pull the wool over a journalist's eyes. That way lies *big* trouble.

So what is the secret of good media relations? It is really very simple and straightforward:

- Take the trouble to find out how the media work.
- Take the trouble to find out the identity of key journalists in the relevant areas as far as the company is concerned.
- Get to know them, get to understand them. Create an open and honest relationship with them. Recognise what they want.
- Recognise, too, the simple fact that if there is news it is their responsibility to get it and no matter how warm a personal relationship may be it must not be allowed to get in the way of this.
- *Never* answer a journalist's question with 'No comment'!

Making the most of the company's case

To communicate the company's record of achievement you must know what it is and have collected the relevant information. Why should you bother? Here are some cogent reasons. First, keeping shareholders and investors informed of your success is part of a pre-emptive approach to guard against an unwelcome takeover. Second, it is good for the morale of those working in the company to know about and be able to share in success; the story about the new order achieved, or about the awkward delivery which was made on time against large odds, helps to build this important element of morale. Third, a successful company is often able to attract the best managers and staff simply because people generally like to be associated with success. It is a very human reaction. Fourth, customers and suppliers also like dealing with successful companies. Finally, those living and working in the community like to know that a prestigious and successful company is in their midst.

Successful communication can be achieved in many ways. The most obvious is the effective use of the Annual Report. Other obvious ways are through the implementation of a special corporate advertising campaign and, perhaps more importantly, through the planning and operation of a special public relations campaign to agreed objectives. It follows that the message of success must be tailored to meet the specific objectives of each target group to which that message is to be delivered, from employees to shareholders.

Other tools to be used to make the company's case include the planning of events programmes, literature and visual aids, and the company's contribution in specialist areas which are described in Part II of this book.

Measuring the results and ensuring value for money

No-one would claim that to measure the results of any communications programme and to ensure that a company is getting value for money is easy. But positive action can be taken which should be helpful. How does the reader set about it?

In order to prove that any specific campaign has caused a change, it is necessary to know what has changed and the degree of that change. This is why a baseline is necessary because then measurement is possible against this. Research is required to capture a 'snapshot' picture of how the company is seen by all of the key target groups.

In establishing the baseline it is necessary to know what should be measured. The three major criteria which should be included are: financial responsibility, ethics, and the social responsibility of the organisation.

Researching financial responsibility will provide information on how the company is seen with regard to its financial soundness and standing. This can be indicated through measures such as market share. It will include influences on investors and on those who recommend investment in the company. The research should provide information on what people know about how the company *gets* its money and *how* it spends it. In this context it is important to recognise that beliefs about an organisation are strongly tied to confidence, trust and loyalty. Is it, therefore, important to measure loyalty? If the company is involved in a takeover the loyalty of investors and shareholders may be critical. The key point here is that traditional measures of financial responsibility most often are not adequate.

Evaluating the company's ethics will indicate the public perception of the company and beliefs about the company. Beliefs about ethics and ethical problems or situations are based in values. Getting sound feedback on how the company is perceived in this key area is central to the company's planning for the future.

Evaluating the social responsibility perception of the company is the third major area of importance. This research should provide information on how all the key target groups see the company as a corporate citizen, good, bad or indifferent. In the words of Doug Newsom:

Social responsibility or good citizenship means producing sound products or reliable services in a way that doesn't threaten the environment, and that compensates employees fairly as well as treats them justly. It means no overpriced, dangerous junk that's called a product. It means no misuse of this small planet and its creatures. It means restoring and protecting what your organisation might threaten in 'normal business operations'. It means treating people who perform your organisation's tasks fairly and justly regardless of the cultural environment in which you operate. Clearly translated that means no slave labour and no discriminatory practices. Social responsibility or social mindedness also means contributing positively to the social political and economic health of a society, whether local or global.

Having got the baseline research, it is important to inaugurate a monitoring system, and to commission regular updates to be made available to management. Very frequently a company will set in motion the procedures required and then fail to create the right set of liaison procedures and meetings to ensure that the information coming into the company from such research and related operations is given the serious time and attention necessary to fulfil the potential of the information.

Finally evaluation of the work of the company and whether this represents value for money will depend on the above and other, specific campaigns, particular to marketing, personnel management and other management functions. It is, of course, necessary to co-ordinate all the information received and to have this discussed in detail by the relevant management committees and groups in the company to mine the information for the data necessary to change any direction or to make other relevant decisions as a result.

In conclusion

- Information is power. In order to use this vital management tool to its maximum potential it is important to look at the information function overall and to update this as necessary to reflect a higher priority.
- Getting the company's message across needs careful planning, to develop the strategic objectives for the communications programme and to ensure these are in tune with the company's corporate objectives and strategy.
- It is very important to consider the subject in the widest sense, from the

corporate identity of the company right through to relationships with all the key target groups.

● Research is an essential component of the communications mix.

● Financial responsibility, ethics and the social responsibility of the company all need to be measured, and monitored regularly.

● There is no 'soft' option. This matter is one of the highest priority for the company. It should be recognised as such at Board level.

CHAPTER 14

Managing a crisis

Achieving good corporate citizenship entails having a comprehensive grasp of the communications functions of the company in order to ensure that the information coming into the company and the information emanating from the company are well and effectively co-ordinated and in harmony with each other. It is important to recognise, too, that the company is sending messages in many directions at once. Managing the communications function, therefore, requires planning and anticipation. This, in turn, means recognising the problems which exist today and diagnosing those that may exist tomorrow.

The essential key to good corporate citizenship is to ensure that the company is kept on an even keel, and, therefore, crisis avoidance must be a central aim. It is the hope of all managements that crises will be avoided. Most enlightened managements, however, recognise the importance of planning for the unexpected which an unlucky fate may decide to deliver!

This chapter will define, illuminate and analyse the anatomy of a crisis, beginning with the early warning stage, when many crises can be recognised and averted. It will identify common denominators and offer guidance on how to manage communications and decision-making during a time of crisis. At this time events can take place with alarming speed and when emotional responses are likely to be heightened with critical and logical faculties at low ebb.

Defining a crisis

What is a crisis? It has been defined by *Webster's Dictionary* as 'a turning point for better or worse', as a 'decisive moment' or a 'crucial time'. In this context it is important to remember that change can be both good or bad. This chapter, however, deals with crisis management when the impending change is likely to have harmful results, prejudicial to the company's future and, perhaps, even to human life itself. It is to be hoped that dealing with a major change likely to produce positive, beneficial results for the company will be easier for management to handle and that they are less likely to need the type of advice on the management of good news to which this book is dedicated!

The essence in defining a crisis is to know the nature and extent of the emergency which may need to be dealt with. Here is a short checklist which may be helpful.

- What is the nature of the problem?
- Is it getting worse?
- When did the emergency start?
- When was its significance recognised?
- What is its history and who has been responsible for dealing with it?
- Is the matter likely to fall under media or government scrutiny?
- What are the risks to business?
- What are the risks to the company?
- Are there any wider spheres of likely risk, and if so, can the risk be identified?
- What is the likely scenario for the future history of the emergency?
- What are the options for likely outcomes?

Crisis typology

Doug Newsom, a distinguished American academic at Texas Christian University, has made a special study of crises. I am indebted to her for the following definition of crisis typology. There are two types of crisis – violent and non-violent. Both types can be subdivided into acts of nature, intentional and unintentional events. Some examples are given in Table 14.1. Violent crises are cataclysmic, immediate and involve loss of life or property. Non-violent crises may be sudden and involve upheaval, but any damage is less tangible and immediate.

The birth of a crisis

The birth of a crisis is when the waves are in the process of formation, soon to increase in number and strength, to create a momentum of their own, to become a flood . . . to threaten to sweep all before them. The signs are there to be seen. The challenge to management is to see them in time. Recognising the birth of a crisis is critical to being able to avoid it or, at least, to contain and manage it.

Table 14.1   Newsom's typology of crisis

	Violent	Non-violent
Act of nature	Earthquakes Forest fires Red tide	Droughts Epidemics
Intentional	Terrorism	Hostile takeovers Insider trading
Unintentional	Explosions Fires Leaks	Stock-market crashes Business failures

The first point of significance to recognise in crisis management is that there is an 'early warning' phase. The persons in the organisation able to diagnose the 'early warning stage' and the telltale critical signs of troubles ahead are those who, overnight, could become the guardian angels or white knights of the company, its heroes.

So, what are the key priorities which the reader should remember in this important area of management? Many would agree that these are:

- The recognition that any time the company is not in a crisis situation it could easily be in an 'early warning' stage of a crisis.
- The company should be alert, vigilant and prepared at all times.
- To be a good corporate citizen the company should ensure that the recognition of this priority is promulgated throughout the company, at all levels, so that the 'guardian angel or white knight' can make himself or herself known to management.
- The company should identify the general nature of likely problem areas and the issues which could be sensitive and result in a full-blown crisis.
- The company should define and create crisis procedure guidelines so that the relevant people in the organisation can know what is expected of them should the need arise.
- The company should recognise that if it is operating in a high-risk area then there is a requirement to share information with others, even competing companies. This policy of open lines of communication through competing companies and even industry groups is essential to help to avoid and contain a crisis.
- The company should also define and recognise the differences between the beginning of a crisis (in the early warning stages), when the crisis can be either avoided or contained, and the crisis itself. At this time the experience has to be lived through – there is no turning back.

Managing a crisis

The first essential in managing a crisis is the recognition of the separate stages: the 'early warning' or 'pre-crisis' stage, which has been already discussed; the acute stage, when the crisis is at its height; and the resolution stage, when the peak has been reached and matters are drawing to a conclusion. However, there can be a vast difference between a conclusion which is resulting in the lessening or calming of the influences which led to the crisis and one which is reached when the crisis is exacting its toll!

During all the above stages, and preferably well in advance of them, there is need for a proper management structure, managing information in and out, and co-ordinating necessary action and responses. Every company, indeed, should have a crisis management plan, and this should relate to separate divisions and departments within the company. There is need for everyone to know what is expected of them, and who to turn to if they need help or advice. This calls for the setting up of a crisis management team.

It may be well to remember the 'boat drill' procedures on a ship or the evacuation procedures which are gone through at the commencement of a flight. These take little time, and less effort but, as a result, every person knows what the procedure is, where to get the necessary equipment, how to use it, and where to get more information if this is needed. The management of a crisis calls for the same, simple type of set procedures and disciplines. Company time and effort spent on such areas is wise investment indeed.

So what are the questions which need to be addressed by the company's crisis management team? These will be many and varied and will, of course, relate to the specific area of the company's operation and the nature of the problem and emergency likely to be encountered. A list of such questions should certainly include the following:

- In managing a crisis, who is responsible for informing employees; for getting help; for informing relevant authorities; and for informing the media?
- What procedures should be followed by those who will field enquiries?
- What are the 'damage limitation' procedures to handle enquiries from families, media, authorities?
- What are the procedures to establish the nature of any rumours about the company in current circulation and to correct or contain these?

Crisis forecasting

It could well be that the help of employees could be sought in the creation of scenarios for crises which the company may have to face. Handled sensitively, such procedures could help unify the company, creating the feeling of 'one team' while, in addition, creating a selection of possibilities for management to consider.

Recent surveys indicate that while the overwhelming majority of managements agree that a crisis in business today is pretty well inevitable, it is only the minority that have prepared crisis management plans. It is, therefore, self-evident that the matter of crisis forecasting – the first step in the preparation of a crisis management plan – is an area for urgent management attention.

Identifying the *type* of crisis which may be encountered is an essential prerequisite to crisis forecasting. Here again the list which the company should prepare will relate to the nature of its business, but the following can provide a checklist for initial consideration:

- Industrial accidents.
- Environmental problems.
- Industrial relations issues (strikes, etc.).
- Product safety.
- Investor relations.
- Hostile takeovers.
- Proxy fights.
- Regulatory authority issues.
- Rumours and media leaks.
- Legislation difficulties or breaches.
- Acts of terrorism.
- Problems related to parliamentary lobbying/pressures.

Controlling communications in a crisis

Essential to good crisis management is the ability to manage the communications element. Controlling the nature of messages from the company is a key ingredient to likely damage limitation. In this context, a company frequently rates its skill in communications more by the news which may be prejudicial to the company's interests and which is not covered by the press or broadcasting media, rather than by those messages beneficial to the company which are given air time or are featured in local, specialist, national or international media.

The time to begin to look at the preparation of the communications plan in relation to the management of a crisis is when there is no crisis! This may seem obvious but, alas, it is still all too rare for management to spend time and effort on this key area.

Here are some priorities for consideration in relation to communications at a time of crisis:

• It has been said before that communications is an ongoing process. Therefore, it must be assumed that the communications machine is in existence and that all key media, parliamentarians and others in important target groups, have an ongoing liaison with the company already established.

• As a consequence of the above, the company's key spokesperson will have been identified. That person's links with top management will have been established. He or she will know the likely damaging effects of statements such as 'No comment' at a time of a major crisis, and the need to avoid such statements.

• Positive information with regard to the company's record will be available. This will cover the key sensitive areas including product and plant safety, non-strike performance, productivity, economic performance and contribution, stability of employment, community involvement, charitable giving and the like. All relevant statistics in all the areas identified as important to the company will have been collated and made available in simple fact-sheet form. Key statements endorsing the company's record, available from independent spokespeople of authority will also have been collected and put into a form suitable for swift and easy use. In particular, any necessary 'blood chits' (permissions for use) will have been obtained so that there is evidence in writing that the statements can be used by the company without reference back to the authors.

In all aspects of managing the communications function in a crisis it is important to respond. It is, therefore, essential to ensure that the company is in a position to *anticipate* what the media may wish to know. They will, naturally, require information which is factual, where accuracy is assured, which is comprehensive, easy to digest and where the sources are authoritative and identified. They will also wish to have background information, including brief personal details about the persons of authority speaking for the company. In addition there could easily be need for photographic material, flow-charts, statistics, historical material and even for special facilities for interviewing executives of the company and employees at shop-floor level. Clearly anyone likely to be in this position will need to have briefing and even training if broadcasting media, such as television, could be involved.

The communications chain

Priorities need to be set as to the order in which particular groups are informed when it comes to a major crisis. Here is a priority list for consideration, with a note of what key information it is important to transmit to each.

- *Employees.* It should be self-evident that this group needs to hear first and immediately if there is a crisis. They need to be given as full, candid and accurate material on the nature and extent of the crisis as is possible, and as quickly as possible. In this context, it should be borne in mind that there will be, inevitably, contact between the media and individual employees. This must not be discouraged. However, it follows that it should be remembered that any written communication may find its way into the hands of the local press or broadcasting station. Clearly the families of the company's employees also need to hear direct from the company just as soon as possible on issues which relate to them (for example, personal injury or safety).
- *Customers.* They need to be told about the crisis with specific reference to how it may affect the business of the company with them. This could include the recall of products, reformulation of products, late delivery of orders, and so on.
- *Stakeholders (shareholders, bankers etc.).* They need to get crisp, accurate information so that they are confident that they know what is going on. It is wise to consider telling them that the company will report to them at identified intervals so that they know that their information will be updated regularly.
- *Opinion formers.* This important group will include regulatory authorities, officials in government, relevant trade and industry bodies, local community leaders, local government, local MPs and MEPs, and the like. They will need to know the nature and extent of the crisis and what is being done about it, in particular they need to be told about damage-limitation plans.
- *Suppliers and those with direct business and professional relationships with the company.* These include the company lawyers, accountants, insurers, suppliers, agents (including advertising agents, market research companies, management or other consultants) and relevant media. They will need to have information on the nature and extent of the crisis and how it is being managed.

There are many methods which can be used to transmit information on a crisis to those it is agreed should receive it. This can be done: by letter; by telephone; by the production and circulation of special 'newsheets' directed at identified target groups; by telex or fax; by electronic mail services; and at specially convened conferences and briefings to relevant small and large groups as necessary.

The implications of stress

In a crisis it is obvious but imperative to recognise the implications of stress. Stress will be present, at varying levels, in all persons with knowledge about the crisis. It is also important to recognise the fact that those who know least about the crisis may suffer the greatest stress as a result of the level of ignorance they are being asked to endure.

Key, too, is the fact that people coping with stress can be volatile and emotional, and liable to act unreasonably and illogically. At a time of stress the process of decision-making becomes difficult. It requires an even more acute level of awareness and vigilance. Stress also calls for recognition from management of its possible limitations of knowledge and experience of how to deal with stress. Many organisations seek help in this area from outside specialists, management consultants or psychologists.

In conclusion

- The chances are that the company will pass through a period of crisis – it may occur in the immediate future.
- It is best to be prepared for a crisis.
- A crisis can be managed, indeed it *has* to be managed.
- There are distinct and differing phases through which a crisis passes. These should be recognised.
- It is important to identify a crisis management team and to prepare and promulgate a detailed crisis management plan so that every member of the company knows that there are detailed procedures and to whom they should report in the event of a crisis.
- Communications play a criticial role in managing a crisis.
- The company must recognise its responsibilities to inform key target groups of a crisis, from its own employees and their families to its customers and shareholders.

PART IV

Conclusion

CHAPTER 15

The way ahead for business

What are the prospects for the business manager in the business and industrial world of the 1990s and in the important early years of the new century? They will be years of considerable political, technological and economic change. The prospect is challenging and also daunting, with different national groupings world-wide setting themselves up for increasing commercial competition. The following components of developing challenge, a small sample, speak for themselves:

- *The environment.* This includes issues such as the ozone layer, the greenhouse effect or global warming, environmental pollution, whether by chemical or other effluent, and noise or related unpleasant and potentially harmful factors. Newspapers, magazines and radio and television programmes deal with these matters almost every day, usually pointing the finger at industry alone. Increasingly frequently the call is understandably for a positive response from business because it is industry that will provide the measures to be taken. Alas, too infrequently the point is made that (as history records) the world is evolving all the time – that the products and services we use have been developed and are provided in good faith, that new and emerging information has drawn attention to the potential hazards, often not realised before, and that the responsible business will always respond but that this takes time, effort and money. Frequently, too, the shrill clamour of the noisy, single-issue pressure groups focuses attention on what is wrong but hardly ever points out the complete consequences of taking the action they are promoting. Too often the public is given the impression that the solution is just to 'stop' the industry actively concerned.

  It is easy enough to cry out against the use of 'chemicals' in food production. What, however, does one give the baby to eat when foods perish quickly or if farmers find that their fields grow healthy pests and weeds but ailing crops? And what will be the cost of the food then? Can it be afforded at all? Also, how fair would it be to ask the Third World, often innocent of the production problems now causing the pollution, to help the developed world pay for the costs of its efforts? 'Let the polluter pay' is a theme being looked at in all seriousness by many governments, including that of the United Kingdom. The sobering example of what befell another European government which tried to embark on this policy is well to the fore in the minds of those grappling with this issue – that government fell within a very few hours! No president, prime minister, national or local politician relishes that prospect ... The director and manager, however, must be aware of the responsibility of the company in these areas and ensure that the company record can stand up to inspection.

- *Third World debt.* This currently stands at some $1.3 trillion. In a world growing 'smaller' by the day as a result of instant communications, what is the extent of businesses' responsibility to help those in other countries, even if they do not trade there? And what should be the nature of this help? The business manager must be clear on what needs to be known, and on how it affects the company's work and its plans for future activities and markets.

- *Political and other changes.* Perestroika and glasnost are with us – good. So are various freer frontiers and other initiatives – also good. There are also reactions against such forms of social progress as happened so sadly in Beijing, China – not so good so far, though there are currently hopes for improvement. The point is that these changes are often sudden, frequently rapid, and usually far-reaching. Confusion, complexity and uncertainty are attributes business have to live with today to a greater extent than hitherto – and their pace of advance may quicken. Rewards of larger markets are attractive; and fears of greater competition and of takeover for asset-stripping may be inhibiting. The better the ethical bases for company activities and the higher the ultimate efficiency of operation, the better will a company be able to evolve into a future in which conventional planning will be increasingly difficult. It will be good corporate citizenship to succeed.

- *Strong religious beliefs.* This is an issue which has already reared its head in many countries of the world. It is already affecting life in countries such as Britain where new first- and second-generation citizens are expecting that their beliefs and approaches to life in general, from their old country, must be recognised, accepted and given priority in their new host country. The manager of the future must know the facts and understand their implications, so that the non-religious consequences, too, can be taken into consideration in planning the company's future.

- *Population explosion.* This is perhaps the most critical issue of all. In some 12 years the population of the planet is expected to rise by another 1 billion. Even today, visitors to cities such as Calcutta, São Paulo, Istanbul, Lima, Mexico City and other similar cities, can see the population explosion and its effects visibly over time periods as short as a year or two. Millions of new citizens are on the streets of these cities and there is also a continuing net drift from the land into the cities. The effects of the population explosion are not only a world issue. They effect the director and company executive, both indirectly and directly. Business, when all is said and done, has to make its contribution to paying for the population explosion, or to controlling it, or to controlling its far-reaching effects. This matter is another which needs to be reviewed and that review needs to be updated, regularly, in the responsible business of tomorrow.

- *Health issues.* These, to include the new communicable diseases, such as AIDS, and the disastrous results of the increase in the use of habit-forming, faculty-destroying drugs – all have implications for the business manager of today as well as of tomorrow. What, for example, should be the company policy with regard to employees and AIDS? Should the company involve itself in a health education programme to ensure employees know about the risks and avoid them? Should the company practise regular compulsory testing for AIDS, related to new employees or existing employees, and/or their families? Does the business of the company risk passing infections on to any section of the public? Should the company redefine its insurances, telling, or perhaps not telling, its employees that it is doing so?

  Even today's boardrooms are beginning to see issues like this one appear increasingly on their agendas as their companies review their roles as good corporate citizens. As time goes by such issues will proliferate.

- *The march of technology.* Already marvellous things are possible – interplanetary travel, increasing understanding of the bases of life, rapid communications, and ultra-rapid calculation and data manipulation, for example. But there are signs that some aspects of technological advance may be outstripping the capacity of most human beings both to understand it properly and to ensure it remains servant rather than becoming master, as well as to comprehend and resolve some of the new ethical conflicts that are arising. Centralised persuasion techniques (to consumers as regards their finances, for example), genetic engineering (in the production of new bacteria or viruses), centralised data banks (for example, of individuals' personal details) and computerised data handling (of money transactions, for instance), are some examples where the problems are already arising. These problems also include the possibility of things going very wrong with consequences difficult to alleviate or correct.

Other important facts – with their accompanying and relevant charts (which follow) – should be borne in mind. They relate to the overall human and social environment of the past, and to that in which the business will be operating in the years to come.

- The proportion of population aged 65 + is predicted to double from a tenth to a fifth of the total population.
- In England and Wales, one-fifth of all marriages would break down within eight years, and nearly two-fifths* of all marriages would ultimately break down (see Figure 15.1).
- Ethnic minorities as a proportion of the population are growing rapidly, particularly in the metropolitan areas (see Figure 15.2).
- Since 1952 average real earnings and personal disposable incomes per head have more than doubled (see Figure 15.3).
- Expenditure on services as a proportion of total expenditure is now rising (see Figure 15.4).
- The borrowing ratio has risen from 4 to 15 per cent since 1970; savings gross of borrowing have remained relatively constant.
- In the 1987 SustainAbility survey of attitudes to environmental performance (SustainAbility is an organisation founded by John Elkington, a well-known conservationist), the financial sector received the worst rating (see Figure 15.5).

Food for thought for the business manager.

Shaping the corporate future

In order to plan for the company's future it is important to recognise such emerging trends as these, and to evaluate what action may be necessary in relation to them.

The culture of the business is important, and changing. We have been passing through the period of the 'power' culture, authoritative and hierarchical, and also through the time of the 'role' or 'bureaucratic' culture, where power is exercised through rules, systems and procedures.

*based on the assumption of 1987 rates remaining constant.

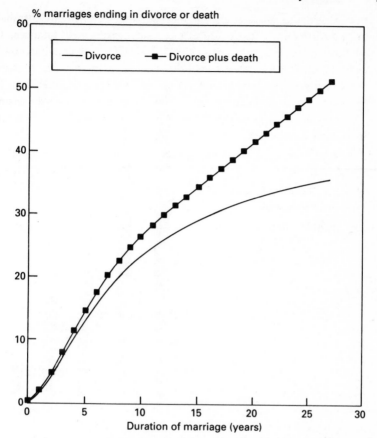

Figure 15.1   Rate of breakdown in marriages. (Source: Office of
Population Censuses and Surveys, *Population Trends* 55, HMSO 1989.)

This latter, too, although apparently different, is also a form of
hierarchical culture. With both these cultures people are motivated by
external factors, perhaps financial or statistical. They are given rewards, in
terms of praise, status, honours or finance, for example. They have fear of
penalties.

These cultures are today regarded as old fashioned. They either have
been replaced or are in the process of being replaced. Company cultures
are now becoming orientated towards 'achievement', or 'support'.

In the 'achievement' culture, the company and its employees are
concerned to 'make a difference to the world' or 'to figure on a page of the
history of the world'. This provides opportunities for members of the

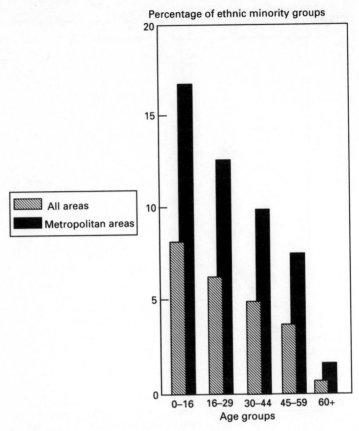

Figure 15.2   Rapid growth of ethnic minorities as a proportion of the population. Figures are an average for 1985–7. (Source: *Labour Force Survey.*)

company to use their talents in ways that are satisfying to them and which contribute to a goal or purpose to which the individual is deeply committed. The emphasis is on action, autonomy, innovation and the shaping of the environment in its widest sense. It makes high demands on members' time and energy and can tend to lead to 'burn-out' in some people, but it can be deeply satisfying on an individual basis. Company managers have, thus, to learn to live with the high levels of stress that may be involved.

The 'achievement' and 'support' culture supports work through close relationships. Employees are being taught interpersonal skills. They learn to trust and care for each other as they learn to trust and care for the

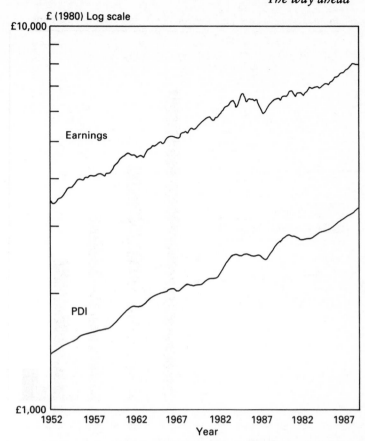

Figure 15.3   Growth of average real earnings and personal disposable income per head.

company. They are responsive and motivated to fulfil their needs within themselves. Rewards are different, including the sense of belonging, and co-operating, and of mutual responsiveness. This brings out in individuals in the company a positive response to the company's customers. Thus, the company is in a strong position to alleviate the pressure on individuals that the strain for achievement can bring with it.

The way ahead for business is to take all these very varied matters seriously, to give them the time, attention and priority they deserve for the sake of the company's future business needs. Also to derive agreed company objectives in these areas and to plan in practical terms towards achieving them; and finally to consider what the following phase(s) of company culture evolution may turn out to be.

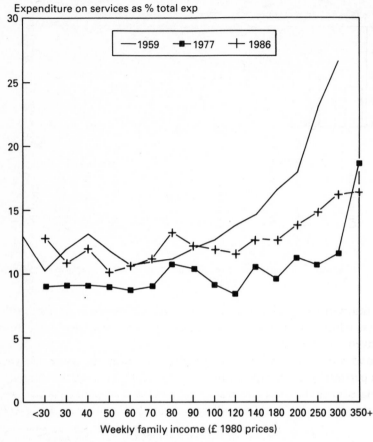

Figure 15.4   Expenditure on services as a proportion of total expenditure. (Source: *Family Expenditure Survey.*)

In summary

This book has endeavoured to give the reader a bird's eye view of what is expected of the company as a 'good corporate citizen'. It has made the case that, in tomorrow's business world, this will be even more important than it is today. It has emphasised that tomorrow's customers will be more discerning, and will increasingly be influenced by a widening range of factors beyond those of saturation, blunderbuss-approach national advertising and brand marketing techniques, common today. The company responding to these factors will be building new markets and extending its existing markets *profitably into the future.*

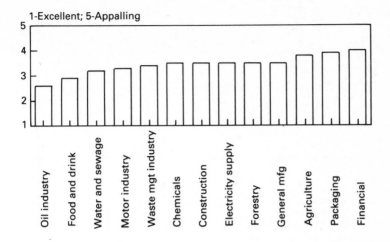

Figure 15.5 Attitudes to environmental performances. (Source: *Green Pages*, SustainAbility, 1987.)

A range of companies is starting to tread this new, ethical road to the success which can emanate from 'good corporate citizenship'. It is still a relatively small band.

Good corporate citizenship is satisfying and rewarding on many levels, both personally and for the business. Every single person in the company, or related with the company in any way, business or personal, likes to feel and share in pride of the overall enterprise. This is a very simple, a very human reaction. It should lead to a more profitable and worthwhile business.

It deserves a try. Try it today.

PART V

Appendices

Appendix I

CASE STUDIES

Case study 1:
a multinational as a corporate citizen

Gaye Pedlow
British American Tobacco Company

BAT Industries plc is one of the world's largest business enterprises, with interests principally in financial services and tobacco.

BAT Industries is well known in the UK for promoting enterprise in the inner cities, notably Brixton, Liverpool and Southampton. In 1988 it won two of the five 'Dragon Awards' given annually to British companies for their work in the community. BAT Industries is also a sponsor of Macmillan College in Teeside, one of Britain's first city technology colleges. Worldwide, Group companies provide support for a wide range of community projects in areas such as education, vocational training, job creation, urban and rural regeneration, medicine and the arts.

This case study looks at one of the Group's tobacco companies, BATCo, with headquarters in London.

The tobacco company

BATCo is the holding company for the BAT Industries tobacco interests in over 40 countries. The major subsidiaries are located in the UK, continental Europe, Latin America, the Caribbean, Asia and Africa, with leading cigarette brands in over 30 countries, such as Benson & Hedges, John Player Special and State Express 555. The company buys and processes tobacco from sources such as the USA and Canada.

In addition, it has pioneered and developed tobacco growing widely in developing countries.

Philosophy and history

BATCo was established as an international company from the start in 1902, originally with no home market, managing overseas and export business from a UK base. The company decided not to become an owner of land or grow its own leaf tobacco, except for experimental purposes. Wherever possible, it promoted the growing of tobacco by independent small farmers; the company now buys tobacco from some 500,000 small farmers every year. Growing areas are frequently remote and it was often necessary to build roads and bridges, provide a water and power supply and other essential services simply in order to be able to operate effectively.

Tobacco is a complex crop to grow, requiring much agricultural expertise; so BATCo companies provide agricultural extension services to farmers to guarantee a good-quality product. Even today, this service often represents the only agricultural training which farmers receive. With large numbers of people in remote, rural areas, it frequently became necessary for the company to provide housing, medical services and schools.

Thus the relationship between BATCo and its local communities is necessarily close. While in the developed world people expect a wide range of services to be available as of automatic right, usually provided by government, there are many places in the world where the local BATCo company is the sole provider of services ranging from clean water supply to the loan of a company vehicle to act as an ambulance. This interdependence of company and community is not viewed as 'good works' or as charity, but as a necessary investment in the future success of the business. The benefits of a good corporate reputation are considerable. 'Enlightened self-interest' is by no means new as a BATCo philosophy.

Types of activity

In 1988 BATCo carried out a world-wide audit of corporate citizenship activities by operating companies, as part of a wider exercise co-ordinated by BAT Industries. Forty BATCo companies reported their overall policies and identified priorities; budget planning and allocation; the management and assessment of activities; the selection of beneficiaries; the nature of the funding or services provided; the cost of human resources and secondments and the ways in which companies communicated their activities to employees or the outside world. The results highlighted some interesting regional variations in the types of activity undertaken.

Within Europe, for example, the main emphasis of company activities is on aid for small business development (34 per cent of total spend) and youth training (23 per cent). Support is therefore clearly geared to job creation and the fight against unemployment.

In Africa, 30 per cent of the total spend on corporate citizenship activities is dedicated to agricultural programmes designed to improve food security. General welfare projects – the provision of services such as water, electricity, the building of roads and bridges, housing projects, and so on – account for a further 20 per cent of total spend.

In Asia, the emphasis is on educational projects (45 per cent), with extensive scholarship schemes being run by companies such as Malaysian Tobacco Company. A further 10 per cent of total spend is dedicated to medical projects, with some companies funding and running medical clinics in remote rural areas.

In Central America and the Caribbean, the local and national charities sector is well organised, calling on 36 per cent of total spend, while in South America support for local cultural activities accounts for 68 per cent of total spend, mainly because of the extensive traditional cultural programme run by the Bigott Foundation in Venezuela.

The audit results confirmed that corporate citizenship and enlightened self-interest are not concepts which have been developed in the UK and the USA and then exported to the Third World, but that, on the contrary, the developed world is only now catching up with ideas which some companies operating in the Third World have been putting into practice for decades. The original paternalistic corporate culture had its advantages, alongside the extended family system which still prevails throughout the developing world, and which puts much of the burden of community care on the family unit, in the absence of public sector services funded by government.

Another factor which influenced BATCo policy was the extent of local need. One example of this was Uganda at the end of the civil war, when the BATCo general manager immediately determined that the company should focus its attention on assistance to orphans, help for the disabled and projects which assisted in the rehabilitation or rebuilding of devastated communities. In Europe, on the other hand, where needs are perhaps not so visible, the links between companies and communities are not as strong and there is the expectation that government will be able to take the load in terms of funding. With the exception of the UK, which had a track record of old-fashioned paternalism long before enlightened self-interest became fashionable, corporate citizenship as a concept has yet to make much impact on Europe.

Many companies reported donations of goods, services and facilities as part of their overall support programme. Beneficiaries of such gifts include hospitals, churches, schools, universities and local charities. The goods provided ranged from cement, waterpipes and paint (Honduras); typewriters, ceiling fans and sewing machines (Bangladesh); telephone switchboards and Land Rovers (Malaysia); and computers surplus to company requirements (Nigeria). Company vehicles are frequently allocated on loan to community organisations and in remote areas will sometimes serve as ambulances.

Secondment is one area where the UK operating company, BAT (UK & Export) leads the way. Several companies reported, however, that major projects tended to take up considerable amounts of management time, even where no official secondment had been made. The agricultural extension staff employed by many BATCo companies could also be viewed as being part-time secondees to the community; while their main function is to ensure the quality of the tobacco crop, the input which they make to agricultural training represents a useful community service.

The projects themselves

The many projects, large and small, fall broadly into the following areas: agriculture and food security; education; support for local cultural activities; and the provision of medical facilities.

Agriculture and food security

An example of an agricultural training project is the establishment by Nigerian Tobacco Company (NTC) of two Young Farmers' Training Centres. The Nigerian government was keen to encourage more young people to take up farming as a living, in order to promote increased production of food crops and to slow the drift of population to the cities. NTC, which buys its tobacco from 17,000 small farmers, was understandably in sympathy with this general aim. The company therefore established two training centres, which offer a 10–12-month course based on a syllabus similar to that covered by Nigeria's agricultural colleges. The company financed the construction of the two centres and meets their running costs. The students pay no fees for tuition or accommodation and are given a small monthly allowance.

NTC receives around 3,000 applications for the 20–30 places currently available on each programme. The Centres are staffed by NTC divisional leaf managers, who take two years out of the mainstream business to teach the trainees – and the company has found that this secondment period can also play an important role in management development for the staff involved. Not more than 20–30 per cent of the students' time is spent in the classroom; each student is responsible for a plot of land, which he farms with maize, soya beans, melon, tobacco and sorghum (a cereal crop) planted in rotation. The vast majority of those trained are now farming for themselves, and the drop-out rate from the courses has been negligible.

BAT Zaire has co-operated with the Food and Agricultural Organisation of the United Nations and with the World Bank on the development of a new, high-yield cassava, which it supplies to small farmers (cassava is a root crop commonly grown for food or as a cash crop throughout the developing world).

In Venezuela, the Bigott Foundation's agricultural extension programme for non-tobacco farmers has resulted in yields per hectare for maize, rice and sorghum which in some areas are almost double the national average.

BAT Mauritius has worked with the government to promote the introduction of new crops to the island, with the aim of reducing the economy's dependence on sugar. The new crops include onions, garlic, ginger, peppers and pistachio nuts. The company provides seeds, fertilisers and technical assistance and runs regional farming competitions in order to publicise the scheme.

In Costa Rica, the Republic Tobacco Company embarked on a small-scale soil-conservation project in 1984, working with a small group of local farmers. The government was so impressed with the results of the company's pilot project that it intends to introduce the scheme on a national basis. It often pays to start small!

Afforestation projects are also an important priority, particularly in parts of the world where wood fuel may be the only source of energy available. The key element in any afforestation project has to be education of both farmers and the community as a whole that wood is not free and that trees which are cut down should be replaced with new growing stock. BATCo-inspired tree-planting programmes are under way in many countries, including Sri Lanka, Bangladesh, Nigeria, Sierra Leone, India, Uganda, Pakistan, Zaire, Honduras, Nicaragua, Zimbabwe and Costa Rica. One of the best examples of a tree-planting programme is that run by BAT Kenya, which has led to 10,000 farmers planting a total of 21 million trees in just under fifteen years.

Education

Support for educational projects falls into two categories: the first is the construction of the school itself; and the second relates to student scholarship schemes.

It is quite common for parents or local businesses in the UK to contribute towards the cost of, for example, a new school swimming pool or science laboratory; however, it is usually taken for granted that the school itself will actually have four walls and a roof. This is not necessarily the case elsewhere in the world. BATCo companies have financed the building of schools in Zaire and Uganda, where BAT Uganda completely rebuilt a secondary school for 500 pupils which had been destroyed in the civil war. In India, Bhadrachalam Paperboards, a subsidiary of a BAT associate company, ITC India, established and runs a school for 1,400 pupils close to its paper mill in Andhra Pradesh.

The Malaysia Tobacco Company introduced a student scholarship scheme in 1955. This proved so successful that the company decided to establish the MTC Foundation in 1982, which took over the administration of the scheme. The Foundation awards scholarships to universities in both Malaysia and the UK, assisting up to 50 students each year. The awards cover full tuition fees, board and lodging, an allowance for books and study materials and one return air passage home every year. Five former scholarship holders are presently employed by the company – one being the current managing director. Because of local graduate employment problems, the scheme has recently been extended in order to offer graduates a year's practical work experience on completion of their degree course.

BATCo's subsidiary company in Chile, Empresas CCT, identified a different sort of educational initiative as a priority and established the Chiletabacos Training Centre in 1985. The Centre provides technical and professional training for underprivileged teenagers about to leave secondary education. Emphasis is placed on the development of basic skills such as hotel services, tailoring, cooking, and so on. So far nearly 300 teenagers have received training and over 75 per cent of those who completed the course have now found suitable employment. In many ways, the scheme is similar in approach to the Project Fullemploy initiative in the UK. Empresas CCT now plans to develop the initiative by offering scholarships to young university students from low-income families who wish to pursue careers in journalism, medicine, agronomy or engineering – all of these being areas related to the company's business interests.

Support for local culture

In Europe and the United States, corporate support for cultural events is sometimes viewed as part of a company's marketing strategy, rather than as support for the community. In other parts of the world, however, preserving cultural traditions and ensuring that they are passed on to the next generation is seen as one way of fostering a sense of national identity, something which is particularly important in developing countries. This was one of the reasons which prompted BAT Kenya to establish and administer a series of regional cultural festivals. These were so successful that the University of Nairobi has now introduced a course specialising in Kenya's traditional culture. In Nigeria, NTC has helped preserve the regional River Festivals, traditionally held in honour of the river gods.

An interesting project is the Art Workshop established by BAT Zimbabwe in association with the National Gallery of Zimbabwe in Harare. In 1982, the company agreed to support a six-month pilot project to provide free art training for youth students. This has now been transformed into a two-year full-time course for over 25 students. The original objective of the Workshop was to contribute to the recreation and redirection of Zimbabwean culture, following the country's independence. Zimbabwean stone sculpture had already earned an impressive international reputation and it was felt that many young Zimbabweans had a great deal of artistic talent. Seven years on, that initial optimism has been justified: the work of the students has received wide critical acclaim and has been exhibited in London, Australia, Norway and Sweden. Five former students have been awarded five-year art scholarships by the Bulgarian government, one student is studying in Sweden and one is pursuing a BA (Honours) degree in fine art at Liverpool Polytechnic in the UK.

On a much larger scale, the Bigott Foundation in Venezuela has established a cultural education centre in the centre of Caracas. Over 1,200 registered members between the ages of five and 60 come to the centre to learn how to play traditional musical instruments and to attend classes on Venezuelan traditional dancing. Aside from the small registration fee, tuition is free and students put on weekly performances for the public in the centre's small theatre.

Medical facilities

Primary health care is a priority need in many developing countries and governments frequently call on BATCo companies for help. In some cases, this may be because of the company's widespread distribution network – often the only one available – which is essential when dealing with national vaccination programmes, for example.

In Sri Lanka, Ceylon Tobacco Company organises regular weekend health activities in association with the Ministry of Health. CTC also assists the Ministry with the production of a protein-rich nutritional compound called thriposha, which is distributed to almost 600,000 undernourished children and nursing mothers every month.

Bangladesh Tobacco Company sponsored the launch of the country's Eye Donation Movement and has provided sustained support for fund-raising campaigns to finance cornea collection and grafting. Pakistan Tobacco Company is currently planning to establish eye clinics close to two of the company's factories.

Finally, an associate company in India, ITC, has been involved with the distribution of contraceptives on behalf of the government for over 20 years. Family planning is a clearly identified national priority and ITC made use of its widespread cigarette distribution network to distribute Nirodh condoms. In 1980, the company suggested to government that their marketing skills might also be of assistance. Since that time, a wide range of marketing techniques has been introduced, including sponsorship of television and radio slots, village festivals and sporting events and a village adoption scheme which brings doctors to remote areas to advise on primary health care as well as on family planning. The overall aim of the marketing campaign has been to reduce the shyness associated with contraceptives and to highlight their social acceptability. Sales of Nirodh by ITC have risen from just over 3 million in 1968 to just under 129 million in 1987. The company received the 1988 award for family planning from the Federation of Indian Chambers and Industry.

Defining the philosophy

Most BATCo companies audited had a Board guideline paper or similar document which sets out their aims and objectives. Many had used a UK headquarters central guideline – the importance of identifying with the needs and aspirations of the individual country. Even companies which have been running corporate citizenship programmes for years sometimes find the concept difficult to put into words, and individual companies have come up with a wide range and variety of definitions. Empresas CCT of Chile expressed their objective as follows: 'To pursue harmony between company and community, since they are mutually dependent and need each other to prosper.' BAT Zaire put it like this: 'To try to ensure that the communities on which we depend have reasonable access to services such as water, schooling, medical assistance, etc., when these are not provided by government and to participate in the upkeep of roads, bridges and infrastructure so that our business can be conducted efficiently.'

Pakistan Tobacco Company draws a distinction in its definition (and in its budget) between donations made 'for company PR purposes' and those which are 'purely charitable'. This distinction allows the company to manage separately long-term charitable projects such as the establishment of the eye clinics, and means that these projects will not suffer if the number of short-term PR demands on the budget is more than anticipated in any one year. It also very cleverly side-steps the one budgeting problem which is common to almost all companies – how to allow for the possibility that the company chairman will suddenly make a promise to the local mayor, such that the company will provide a new roof for the village hall, half-way through the budget year, without taking funds away from the real priorities.

Perhaps the most comprehensive and most thoughtful definitions of corporate citizenship were those from Pakistan, and also from the West Indian Tobacco Company (WITCO) in Trinidad, both small companies, but leading the field in this respect. WITCO's aims and objectives cover environmental conservation, the need to be sensitive to social and economic change and the need to involve employees in the company's community projects. WITCO also draws attention to some additional considerations which face multinational companies: 'to be seen to balance the use, where necessary, of the expertise of expatriate employees with the need to develop the experience of local employees . . . and to increase public understanding of the role of private enterprise – both its benefits and its responsibilities – with particular reference to the role of multinational companies in developing economies'.

Central and local initiatives

The operating companies could perhaps claim that they have taught the central HQ substantially more about corporate citizenship, simply by getting on with it in practice, than the HQ has communicated to them from the centre. BATCo's decentralised structure means that local management takes the decisions and bears the responsibility for corporate citizenship programmes, just as it does for other aspects of the company's operations.

Various points based on experience over the years, however, can be usefully included in a practical checklist for companies interested either in setting up a corporate citizenship programme for the first time or in trying to assess where they stand with their existing programmes.

- Make sure the proposed programme is really relevant to the needs and aspirations of the local or national community.
- Be selective. Focus on one or perhaps two of those needs, instead of trying to tackle all of them at once. The company may benefit more if it 'specialises' in one area of community activity with which it can be clearly identified.
- Try to choose projects which make use of a company's existing skills and expertise.
- Plan a community programme as professionally as any business project – establish clearly in advance the aims and objectives, ensure that there is an effective way of monitoring or measuring the results on a regular basis and make sure that the objectives which you have set are achievable in practice.
- Evaluate in advance the amount of management time and effort which will be required – it is all too easy to estimate the financial costs but to forget about the other resources needed, and on a large-scale project the time commitment can be considerable.
- Establish proper management and financial controls. Some companies choose to do this by having project committees, which meet regularly to review progress against objectives and to determine future activities. In some of the smaller BATCo companies, it is the general manager who takes the lead and provides the control.
- As with all business projects, there is a greater chance of success if top management is seen to be committed to the programme.
- If the programme demands that the company works alongside a voluntary organisation, recognise that there may be significant differences in approach, or in attitudes to plans, budgets and reporting structures. Lay down the management and financial standards considered to be absolutely essential, but be prepared to be flexible as regards everything else. There is much that the corporate world can learn from the voluntary sector, as well as the other way round.
- Avoid the temptation to rely merely on 'chequebook giving'. Programmes which include assistance in kind – secondment of staff, donations of surplus equipment, provision of technical expertise – can be even more valuable to the community.
- Decide in advance the sort of publicity that is desired and plan how to achieve this. Define the audiences and determine the best means of getting the message across – company newsletters for employees, annual reports for shareholders, local press or radio for small-scale sponsorships, national press or television for major events. In some parts of the world or for certain projects, widespread self-publicity

would go against local customs, but there is usually at least one audience (perhaps the local MP or the appropriate government ministry) which ought to be made aware of the company's contribution.

- Leave some flexibility in the budget planning so that unexpected demands do not mean that other projects have to suffer. Some BATCo companies make special provision for disaster relief projects. Following the 1988 floods in Bangladesh, for example, the local company provided 600 farmers with rice paddy seeds and sank 25 tubewells in order to provide fresh water for 33 villages, all within ten days.
- Build into the system a means of checking progress. BATCo chose to do this by questionnaire, in order to take an up-to-date snapshot of their companies' activities. After a given period of time it would be sensible to follow up with further progress checks, building in any necessary shifts of emphasis.
- Finally, be prepared on occasion to learn by mistakes. Not every project will be a resounding success every time, but if the basic approach is right, it will pay dividends in the long run.

Conclusion

Cynical observers may ask what is in it for BATCo, given that none of the programmes outlined will actually lead to increased sales of their cigarettes. That was not the intention. Like any other company, BATCo can operate more effectively and profitably if the communities in which its subsidiaries are based and from which they draw their employees, are stable and prosperous. There is, however, more to it than that.

Multinational companies are viewed with suspicion in some countries – it is up to them to make it clear by their actions that they are there for the long term and that their contribution to the economy and to the general well-being of local communities is of the highest possible standard. This multinationals can do in several ways – through the terms and conditions of service which they offer to employees, for example. BATCo's corporate citizenship programmes are part of this overall strategy.

BATCo has been operating in the Third World since its establishment in the early days of the twentieth century. The first office in Singapore, for example, opened in 1903 and the first office in Mombasa, Kenya, opened in 1907. BATCo believes that one of the main reasons why the company has been so successful is its long-term commitment to these countries. The track record which has been established as a socially responsible, apolitical and trustworthy employer has proved invaluable in dealings with governments world-wide and has undoubtedly contributed to the success of the international business.

Case study 2: a service company as a good corporate citizen

David Holtom
Radio Rentals

Radio Rentals was established in 1928 in Brighton by Percy Perin-Thoms, who started by renting 'wireless sets'. Some of the first TV sets were actually installed as early as 1939, by which time Radio Rentals had become the world's largest renting organisation.

The company has a firm commitment to 'customer service', 'staff care', and a socially responsible attitude to the community at large. Its customer service commitment was set out in a company brochure published in 1938 as follows:

Service is the foundation of the greatness of Radio Rentals . . . whose satisfied subscribers depend on us for never failing entertainment.

It is service which has earned us a nationwide reputation and given us supremacy, a service built up on scrupulous attention to the needs of those who have made us responsible for their listening, a service which brings us a daily increase in the numbers of our subscribers and one which we shall always strive to maintain.

Every set supplied by Radio Rentals is tested three times, twice in our factory by skilled operatives and once immediately after it is installed in your home.

As a Radio Rentals subscriber you are never – even for a single day – without your radio. In the event of a breakdown, a postcard or telephone call brings immediate assistance from our local engineer and should the trouble necessitate the removal of your set, an identical model from the stock always carried by our engineer will be installed free of cost.

Radio Rentals has set a high ideal of service and our policy will not permit the slightest deviation from it, for we are convinced that our success lies in having none but satisfied customers.

This commitment, though couched in the somewhat grandiose terms of the time, nevertheless remains to this day.

The company staff handbook of 1985 updates this commitment and widens it to include staff care and wider responsibilities.

The following values will govern the behaviour of the company and its management in all dealings with employees, customers and the public at large. . . .

CARING AND FRIENDLY
The company expects management to be caring and friendly in the treatment of staff and for management and staff to display the same characteristics in dealing with customers, prospective customers and other employees.

ETHICAL, MORAL AND LEGAL
It is the company's wish to be ethical, moral and legal in its behaviour to all persons at all times.

SOCIALLY RESPONSIBLE
The conduct of the company will be socially responsible to all the communities in which it trades.

NO UNFAIR DISCRIMINATION
The company will not discriminate unfairly in its approach to customers, prospective customers and employees. In particular it will be an equal opportunities employer and will not discriminate unfairly in matters of recruitment, selection, training, development or promotion in relation to sex, marital status, colour, race, creed or ethnic origins.

DEVELOPMENT OF PEOPLE
The company will provide an environment in which employees are encouraged to develop their talents and abilities and thereby increase their satisfaction and rewards and their contribution to company objectives.

OPEN AND PARTICIPATIVE STYLE
The company will operate an open, honest and participative management style which provides for effective two-way communication and consultation of all matters which effect employees.

MEASUREMENT AND PERFORMANCE REVIEW
The performance of all employees and business units will be frequently reviewed against established criteria.

REWARDS FOR HIGH PERFORMANCE
The company will introduce reward systems which reflect the level of performance achieved.

SAFE AND ACCEPTABLE WORKING ENVIRONMENT
The company will provide working conditions which are appropriate to its position in the market place which, as far as is reasonably practicable, do not endanger the health and safety of employees.

These ideals were further refined and incorporated into the Radio Rentals 'Mission Statement' which again focuses on quality products, services and flexible added value deals which satisfy customer needs.

The emphasis on quality is fundamental to the Radio Rentals philosophy, aimed at achieving long-lasting relationships with its customers. To achieve this requires a clear focus on customers' needs and aspirations. It is not something which can be achieved overnight, it requires a set of attitudes and beliefs which permeate the company culture. It relies on over 6,000 people – many of whom are working on their own visiting customers' homes and therefore not subject to close supervision – clearly understanding the company's 'service philosophy' as there are over 80,000 contacts with Radio Rentals prospective (or existing) customers every working day, any one of which can either enhance or detract from the Radio Rentals service reputation.

To achieve these customer service goals it is clear that not only must the staff selection procedures be right so as to ensure that only individuals with the appropriate attitudes and interpersonal skills are recruited but also comprehensive training is provided to ensure these skills are developed and policies fully understood. Furthermore, it is important to ensure that the 'organisation' itself is structured in a way that ensures that it can respond effectively to customer needs. This service culture focuses on three key areas – commitment, competence and consistency – and can best be summed up by the following qualitites:

- A focus on commitment rather than rules.
- An emphasis on consultation and involvement in two-way communications across levels and functions rather than directives.
- Involvement of all staff in the decision-making and policy formulation process encouraging bottom-up planning rather than top-down policies and directives.
- A communication system which focuses on information and advice rather than instructions and orders.
- Encouraging individuals to take ownership of problems and problems are not passed upwards, downwards or sideways as someone else's responsibility!
- A sense of the value of individuals, based on their achievements and expertise rather than rank.

- A focus on getting things done by using informal relationships rather than a traditional formal organisation structure.
- Encourage individuals to concentrate on doing the right things rather than only on doing things right!
- Provision of customer service by small teams which focus on achieving 'customer satisfaction goals' and group 'commercial targets' rather than on individual objectives.

The way the company is structured reflects the very real customer orientation – it has become less formal and more flexible and responsive. The flexibility of the organisation enables a quick response in a rapidly changing marketplace where both new technology and customers' needs and aspirations require prompt attention.

The achievement of the goals requires high-calibre people who have the opportunity to prove their skills and expertise through carefully structured personal training programmes.

Training and development

The company recognises that the calibre and competence of staff is one of the main factors which will ensure Radio Rentals remains a highly successful company giving first class service to its customers. This is why the company applies a great deal of effort and resource to the provision of high-quality training programmes conducted on and off the job by qualified trainers.

Quarterly performance reviews and an annual appraisal are conducted by the immediate manager as a result of which individual training needs can be identified and action plans agreed to improve job skills and job performance. Every member of staff can therefore be fully involved in the planning, progression and evaluation of training required.

Induction training

It is of prime importance that all new staff understand the company, its values and objectives and the part they will play in making their contribution to customer service. For most staff this initial training takes place off the job but under the guidance of experienced managers who are very familiar with the duties and tasks to be performed.

Occupational skills

Radio Rentals recognise the importance of keeping touch with latest developments in all fields of work. Managers and staff are encouraged to attend appropriate courses either at the divisional training centre group training school or relevant external training courses. Additional divisional training departments are staffed by qualified training managers who keep up to date with developments in modern methods and techniques of training and education.

Relevant education

As a large company, Radio Rentals recognises it has a particular responsibility to the young people it employs. Any young person under 18 years of age who wishes to pursue a course of education through day release facilities will be entitled to do so, provided that the course content is relevant to his or her career with Radio Rentals.

Similarly, adult staff will be encouraged to follow job-relevant courses of evening study at further education centres, where such courses lead to higher-grade and professional qualifications relevant to the business. The company will, by prior arrangement, reimburse tuition and examination fees and may contribute to the cost of textbooks.

Development, promotion and transfer

Suitable candidates are also encouraged to take external degree, diploma or certificate courses with company funding. The company believes that most staff are keen to develop their talents and abilities to the full so that they can obtain maximum enjoyment and fulfilment in their work. The company also believes that managers have a key responsibility in this respect which is met through a system of development appraisals conducted for staff with identified potential for advancement. In this way staff are able to make known their ambitions, ideas and feelings about their work so they can be given all the help and training necessary to enable them to progress along their agreed career paths.

Consultation

As a progressive, forward-looking company, Radio Rentals believes that consultation is essential to the success of every company and is even more vital in a highly competitive service organisation in which a large number of people are employed. The fact that the workforce operates in comparatively small groups from locations spread throughout the UK means that it is vital that staff have the opportunity to contribute ideas, opinions and feedback on company values, policies, procedures and activities. Each division has, therefore, established facilities for consultation to supplement those already available through the line management structure and all employees are encouraged to participate.

Appraisals and reviews

Staff appraisal or performance review systems have been operating in the company for many years and provide employees with the opportunity to discuss with their managers any matters which concern them. The more formal objectives of the management performance review process can be summarised as follows:

1. To identify individual strengths and weaknesses in job performance by focusing on *how* a manager performs.
2. To identify the areas in job performance where action is required by the individual manager, and where additional training is required to enable improvement to take place.
3. To identify realistic development opportunities and assess the potential of the individual manager to take advantage of these opportunities in the short, medium and longer term.
4. To encourage the manager to want to develop his or her full potential and maintain professional standards.
5. To obtain an accepted 'contract' regarding training and development between the manager and the company.
6. To obtain the commitment of managers to the training and development of those for whom they are responsible.

Progress against objectives agreed during the annual appraisals under this process is reviewed at quarterly intervals.

The appraisal and review system used in the case of non-managerial staff is a simplified procedure. It is also designed, however, to review the strengths and weaknesses of past performance and to reach agreement in the ways in which any shortcomings can be overcome. It also provides the opportunity to identify those with the ability to obtain further advancement in the company and to plan the way in which this can be achieved.

Grievance and disciplinary procedures

Should things go wrong, procedures have been introduced to ensure that all staff are treated in a fair and consistent manner. Disciplinary action is never taken without reference to a more senior level and consideration is given to all relevant circumstances, including length of service, previous conduct and performance. Grievances are dealt with as near to the point of origin and as quickly as possible. In the event of an unsatisfactory outcome the member of staff has the right to appeal to higher levels of management and ultimately to the managing director. Members of a union may elect to be represented on an individual grievance by an official of the EETPU or EESA.

Health and safety

It is a fundamental principle of Radio Rentals company policy that the health, safety and welfare at work of all employees are a management responsibility ranking equally with every other aspect of the working day. All managers are directly responsible for ensuring that their duties, as defined in the Health and Safety at Work Act 1974, are carried out and that safe conditions of work are provided and that adequate training is given to enable each employee to work safely and efficiently.

Safety officers have been appointed in each division who are responsible through the personnel director to the Board of directors for ensuring the effective implementation of the company's safety policy to all management and staff. All staff are given a 'Passport to Health and Safety' and managers and safety representatives have been trained in health and safety matters to ensure high standards at all times.

Benefits and services

Among the benefits provided to staff are sickness benefit scheme and holiday bonus based on length of service, a private medical care scheme, personal accident insurance and a savings-related share option scheme. Social subsidies are also provided to enable local managers to provide Christmas parties, dinner dances, and other social events. The company also provides long service awards and a retirement gratuity for full-time employees. The company will also allow reasonable time off with pay to individuals who assist in community activities and certain public duties, including JPs, members of local authorities, health authorities or members of managing bodies of educational institutions or governing bodies.

Wider interests

Although Radio Rentals' primary interest is in providing an excellent service to its customers and a working environment where employees can

realise their potential and reap the rewards of high individual performance, it does recognise a wider set of responsibilities. In making a
considerable commitment to developing the business and its people by not
only concentrating on present needs but also investing for future continual
growth, it recognises its responsibility towards *all* its stakeholders.

Beyond this, it acknowledges and takes very seriously its commitment to
the wider community. Through the parent group, Thorn-EMI, employees
are encouraged to participate actively in charitable giving. Employees are
free to contribute to any charity they wish under the company's scheme. If
they choose to give money to either of Thorn-EMI's chosen charities of the
year (currently Save The Children and the Home Farm Trust) the company
will match the donation pound for pound. In common with other group
companies, Radio Rentals has raised money for the ITV telethon in 1988
as well as Comic Relief and Children in Need. Local divisional activity has
resulted in contributions to many local charities and worthy causes.

Radio Rentals also places a high premium on the value of educational
sponsorships by providing financial assistance to young people and
enabling them to extend their horizons and expand their experience. A
number of students have been able to take advantage of sandwich courses
offered by universities and polytechnics in the UK, which combine three
years of study with a year spent working in the company. Local managers
are encouraged to liaise with local authorities, polytechnics and business
schools, particularly those where members of the management or staff are
taking external courses. Members of the management and training
departments also work with academics on research projects and senior
managers are also encouraged to participate in external conferences and
seminars as speakers, and to hold office in professional or educational
organisations.

Radio Rentals is keen to reduce environmental pollution and, in line
with other Thorn-EMI companies, has converted its fleet of vehicles to
unleaded petrol. Recently a scheme has been introduced to reduce waste
by introducing waste paper recycling at company headquarters.

Case study 3: 'Sheffield partnership in action'
Richard D. Field OBE

For some one hundred years steel production in Britain had risen, then between 1970 and 1980 the industry cut back production from 28.4 to 11.4 million tonnes – a reduction of 60 per cent.

Sheffield industry had to cut back its costs to survive; its major cost was labour. Between 1976 and 1986 the city's unemployment level increased from three percentage points below the national average to three percentage points above it. It peaked in July 1986 at 16.7 per cent.

While business reduced its costs and shed much of its labour force, the City Council increased its costs. It sees itself as a 'caring' Council; thus it saw the care of those without jobs as a priority. It took on a larger workforce and ensured that the Council's services in the community were maintained. The effects upon the city were dramatic, with rates increased by 30 and 40 per cent in two consecutive years. Business and the Council fought with each other through the media. The investors and the business world turned their backs on Sheffield. Those were very dark days.

In January 1986 the City ran five one-day workshops called 'The Challenge and Privilege of Leadership'. Twenty leaders attended each day, including MPs, councillors, business people, bishops, trade unionists, community organisations and the police. Two surprising conclusions came out of these five days: that all who attended had a great pride in Sheffield; and that all wanted to do more but did not know what to do.

Industry Year provided that opportunity to do something: by the end of 1986 more than 2,000 events had been run involving tens of thousands of Sheffielders. Those concerned, from their different points of view, were beginning to work as a team, in the same direction, and their regular meetings ensured that adversaries were becoming friends.

To ensure that the impetus was maintained and increased, the Sheffield Economic Regeneration Committee (SERC) was formed in January 1987. It has some 30 members who meet monthly and are drawn from business, national and local government, the University, the Polytechnic, the local education authority and the wider community.

Although SERC has no power as such, it acts in a co-ordinating capacity, giving support and direction. The Committee raised the money and commissioned a strategy to be produced for the East End of Sheffield; this strategy document, once agreed, became the basis upon which the government set up the Urban Development Corporation which, incidentally, has a unique working agreement with the City Council and a community director to work jointly for the good of the city. SERC has also produced, after consultation, a strategy for the city – 'Sheffield Vision' – to give direction to all that is done. Also in 1987, business and the Council formed 'Partnership in Action', which in 1988 became Sheffield Partnerships Limited. Through this forum business and local government work together to improve the city.

Sheffield's greatest success to date must be the winning of the bid to host the 1991 Universiade (World Student Games), the second largest multi-sport and cultural event in the world. Together Sheffielders presented their bid in Zagreb, together they hosted the decision-makers in Sheffield and together they will host the Games in July 1991

The winning of the bid means more than just the Games, enormous though they are. It means a return of Sheffield's belief and pride in itself. It puts Sheffield, England's fourth largest city, back on the map. In 1991 Sheffield will be the centre of world sport; its sporting facilities will become some of the best in Europe.

So what is different in the city of Sheffield? What does it now have that it did not have before the Partnership? In 1985 it had few if any building projects; now it has over £2 billion's worth, including: the massive and magnificent Meadowhall Centre, retail shopping centre beside the M1 motorway; the canal basin development; the Science Park; the Sheffield Technology Park; Tudor Square, with four theatres including the Crucible and a refurbished Lyceum theatre; and an Olympic standard swimming complex (Ponds Forge). Sheffield has seen the formation of Britain's first regional Per Cent Club, whose member businesses give a percentage of profits to community projects; a city-wide business education partnership which includes the largest compact in Britain and a regional bank – Hallamshire Investments.

Here are some of the lessons that have been learned:

- That the regeneration of the city is a unifying force for good.
- That teamwork, direction and regular meetings are of the utmost importance.
- Excitement is the key to getting people involved and committed.
- Committed 'doers' exist throughout the Community. Find them, use them. As success grows so does their number.

Appendix II

CODES OF PRACTICE

OFT codes of practice

One of the most interesting provisions of the Fair Trading Act 1973 laid upon the Director-General of Fair Trading the duty to 'encourage relevant trade associations to prepare, and to disseminate to their members, codes of practice for guidance in safeguarding and promoting the interests of consumers in the United Kingdom'. There are now many of these codes, published by various trade associations in consultation with the Office of Fair Trading. The range of goods and services covered is wide and various – for example, domestic electrical appliances, motor vehicles, shoes, and holidays. The 1980 Annual Report of the Director-General of Fair Trading stated: 'The aim of codes of practice is to provide a straightforward practical and inexpensive way of improving trading standards by non-legislative means.'

These codes of practice have at their core a model complaints-handling mechanism. Ideally, codes eventually lower complaint rates; failing that, they should at least ensure that complaints are handled better. The major responsibility for resolving complaints remains with the individual company subscribing to the code. Only in the event of a failure to agree between consumer and individual trader do the conciliation mechanisms of the trade association become involved.

SOME CODES OF INTEREST

Unit Trust Customer Code

Introduction

The unit trust industry has some £55 billion under investment, nearly five million accounts and approximately two million private investors. Unit trusts are a popular way for small investors to save and invest in equities – offering simplicity and security and the benefits of expert fund management. Customer care is a high priority in the growing financial sector. This Customer Code of Practice outlines the obligation of those who sell unit trusts and the private investors who buy them. Its aim is to give personal investors in unit trusts simple, clear information as a basis for investment decisions. It has been developed through the Customer Standards Committee of the Unit Trust Association. The Association's membership covers 90 per cent of the industry. All members are committed to respecting the Code. Compliance with it is monitored by the Association on a continuing basis – including complaints records – to ensure that the service provided to personal investors is efficient, courteous and fair. The results of this monitoring process are published annually by the Association in January of the following year.

The role of the Unit Trust Association

The Unit Trust Association was formed in 1959 as the Association of Unit Trust Managers, changing its name in 1976 to reflect its activities on behalf of unitholders as well as its members. Membership of the Association is open to any management company of a UK authorised unit trust. The Association recognises that the growth of the unit trust industry depends on maintaining the confidence of the public. It was formed to maintain the highest standards of practice throughout the industry and this remains an important part of the UTA's role which is to:

1. Agree standards and practices among its members for the protection of the unitholder and to maintain the good name of the industry.
2. Promote the unit trust industry and speak on its behalf to all relevant Government departments and other organisations on matters affecting the industry.
3. Provide information on unit trusts to members of the public, the media and any other enquirer.
4. Act in co-operation with other organisations on matters connected with investor protection.

General obligations on all member companies of the UTA

Members of the Association are required, *inter alia,* to comply with and to be bound by the Unit Trust Customer Code. Members who do not comply with the Code are subject to the Association's disciplinary procedures, as set out in the UTA's Constitution, which can result in suspension or expulsion.

In addition, UTA member companies are to:

1. Conduct business lawfully, comply with all relevant legislation and regulations, and trade fairly and responsibly in the day-to-day conduct of business.
2. Provide appropriate training for staff, in particular in the principles of this Code and compliance with it.
3. Notify the Association of any matters which might adversely affect the reputation of the industry or of the Association.

Specific obligations in dealing with personal investors

UTA member companies will:

1. Comply with all relevant legislation and regulations.
2. Use plain English.
3. Where appropriate, offer potential customers a copy of the Scheme Particulars and the latest annual manager's report and half-yearly report (unless superseded by an annual report) of the unit trust in which they are interested.
4. Publish cancellation, redemption and issue prices for every dealing day.
5. Provide all required documentation promptly.
6. Give best advice within their range of products.
7. Meet specific regulations for advertising. These vary according to the category of advertisement. For example, those which are very general, those which invite you to find out more by writing or phoning, and those which invite you to send money and buy. In general, advertisements must:

   • Not be misleading.
   • Make fair comparisons.
   • Give warnings that past performance is not a future guarantee.
   • Not make claims about being tax-free if the fund is taxable.
   • Give clear details of the period during which cancellation of your intended investment is possible.
   • Give risk warnings about likely fluctuations in capital value.
   • Not give guarantees of fund performance.

8. Make clear in their literature the costs or charges involved, including any commission payable to intermediaries.

9. Send six-monthly and annual reports of any fund in which the customer is a registered unitholder, and to holders of bearer certificates on request.
10. Make settlement for redeemed units within five working days of receipt of all necessary documentation.

The obligations of the personal investor

The only legal obligation of personal investors is to pay promptly for any units they have ordered whether in writing or by phone, personally or through an independent financial adviser. However, it is helpful if they:

1. Notify any change of address.
2. Keep certificates and contract notes in a safe place.
3. Cast their vote when asked.
4. Arrange for registrars to be notified in case of death.

A unit trust, like all trusts, is governed by a Trust Deed. This appoints a Trustee, usually a bank or large insurance company, which holds all the assets so the fund manager cannot make off with the money. Trustees must report to the unitholders that everything has been done in accordance with the Trust Deed and that the regulations of the Securities and Investments Board (SIB) have been met.

It should be noted that a unit trust management company can be taken over by another company without the unitholders being consulted, although unitholders have the power – given sufficient consensus – to remove the managers.

How to complain

If you have a problem it can usually be solved quickly if you take the following steps:

1. Write or phone the unit trust management company stating clearly what is wrong. Give as much information as possible together with your full name, address, name of fund and unit certificate number. Keep a copy of your letter or note of your phone call, such as time, date and to whom you spoke.
2. If you remain unsatisfied after the complaint has been investigated by the company at senior level, you may refer the complaint to the appropriate regulatory body which is identified in the manager's literature or to the Unit Trust Ombudsman if the company is a member of the Ombudsman Bureau. (The appropriate regulatory

bodies are: the Securities and Investments Board (SIB) for those registered directly with it; the Investment Management Regulatory Organisation (IMRO) for complaints about investment management and the Life Assurance and Unit Trust Regulatory Organisationn (LAUTRO) for complaints about marketing.)

The UTA can provide advice about the complaints procedure. It should be noted that the use of any of the routes outlined above does not prevent a complainant from seeking redress through the courts.

Code of Conduct and supporting Guides to Good Management Practice of the British Institute of Management

Introduction

The British Institute of Management was established in 1947 and is an independent, non-party political and non-profit-making organisation. One of its primary aims is to promote the highest professional standards of management. This Code of Conduct forms an essential part of that aim.

All Companions, Fellows and Members are expected to support the aims of the Institute and are bound to uphold the standards prescribed in this booklet.

This document falls into two parts. The Code of Conduct is mandatory upon every manager who becomes a member of the Institute. The Articles of the Institute provide that any alleged breach of the Code may be examined by a committee of Council set up for the purpose and any member found to be contravening any section of the Code is liable to disciplinary action which may result in exclusion from membership of the Institute. The supporting Guides to Good Management Practice amplify this Code.

The Institute's Professional Standards Committee keeps the Code and Guides under regular review.

Code of Conduct

At all times a member shall uphold the good standing and reputation of the British Institute of Management, and in exercising authority as a manager shall:

(a) Comply with the law.
(b) Respect the customs and practices of any country in which he works as a manager.

(c) Not misuse his authority or office for personal or other gain.

(d) Observe the standards prescribed in the Guides to Good Management Practice approved by Council.

This Code of Conduct forms part of a by-law made under Articles 10, 11 and 12 of the Articles of Association of the British Institute of Management. It prescribes the standards which any committee established by Council for the purpose may take into account in considering the conduct of a member of BIM: but so that the committee shall not be prevented from taking other matters into consideration. Any member contravening any section of the Code may be liable to disciplinary action which could result in expulsion from the Institute.

Note

When working outside the United Kingdom the professional manager shall:

(a) Wherever practicable comply with the professional standards set out in the Code and Guides.

(b) Not necessarily be deemed to be in breach of his obligation as a member of BIM if he complies with local custom and practices which are well established but inconsistent in detail with the Code and Guides.

Guides to Good Management Practice

I. AS REGARDS THE INDIVIDUAL MANAGER
   The professional manager should:
   (a) Make proper use of the resources available to him.
   (b) Appraise his own competence, acknowledge potential weaknesses and seek relevant qualified advice.
   (c) Take every reasonable opportunity to improve his professional capability.
   (d) Be objective and constructive when giving advice or guidance in his professional capacity.
   (e) Accept accountability for the actions of his subordinates as well as for his own.
   (f) In pursuing his personal ambitions, take account of the interests of others.
   (g) Never maliciously injure the professional reputation, or career prospects of others nor the business of others.

(h) Be aware of and sensitive to the cultural environment within which he is working.

2. AS REGARDS THE ORGANISATION
    The professional manager should:
    (a) By leadership, co-ordination, personal example and commitment direct all available efforts towards the success of the enterprise.
    (b) Apply the lawful policies of the organisation and carry out its instructions with integrity.
    (c) Define and maintain an organisation structure, allocate responsibilities and encourage the achievement of objectives, by team work where appropriate.
    (d) Demonstrate his loyalty to the organisation by promoting its interests and objectives.
    (e) Promote effective communications within the organisation and outside it.
    (f) Make immediate and full declaration of any personal interests which may conflict with the interests of the organisation.
    (g) Refrain from engaging in any activity which impairs his effectiveness as a manager.
    (h) Act in accordance with his own judgement in any instance of conflict of interest arising from his membership of a trade union, trade association or other body.
    (i) Ensure that plant, processes and materials committed to his charge are maintained and operated as efficiently and safely as reasonably practicable.

3. AS REGARDS OTHERS WHO WORK IN THE ORGANISATION
    The professional manager should:
    (a) Strive to minimise misunderstanding and promote good relations between all who work in the organisation.
    (b) Consult and communicate clearly.
    (c) Take full account of the needs and problems, ideas and suggestions of others.
    (d) Ensure that all his subordinates are aware of their duties and responsibilities especially in relation to those of others.
    (e) Encourage the improved performance of his subordinates and the development of their potential, by means of training and in other suitable ways.
    (f) Be concerned in the working environment for the health, safety and well-being of all, especially those for whom he is responsible.

(g) Promote self-discipline as the best form of discipline both for himself and for his subordinates.

(h) Ensure that disciplinary or other corrective action is constructive and respect the dignity of all concerned.

(i) Using his judgement, advise senior colleagues in advance of situations in which they are likely to become involved.

4. AS REGARDS CUSTOMERS AND SUPPLIERS

The professional manager should:

(a) Ensure that the requirements of customers and suppliers are properly considered.

(b) Ensure that all the terms of each transaction are stated clearly.

(c) Ensure that customers and suppliers are informed of any action which may materially affect the terms of transaction and take all reasonable action to minimise risk to the parties involved.

(d) Avoid entering into arrangements which unlawfully inhibit the process of open competition.

(e) Respect the confidentiality of any information if so requested by customers and suppliers.

(f) Establish and develop with customers and suppliers a continuing and satisfactory relationship leading to mutual confidence.

(g) Neither offer nor accept any gift, favour or hospitality intended as, or having the effect of, bribery and corruption.

(h) Accept or deliver the product or service within the quality, quantity, time, price and payment procedures agreed.

5. AS REGARDS THE ENVIRONMENT, NATURAL RESOURCES AND SOCIETY

The professional manager should:

(a) Recognise his organisation's obligations to its owners, employees, suppliers, customers, users, society and the environment.

(b) Make the most effective use of all natural resources and energy sources for the benefit of the organisation and with minimum detriment to the public interest.

(c) Avoid harmful pollution, and wherever economically possible, reprocess or recycle waste materials.

(d) Ensure that all public communications are true and not misleading.

(e) Be willing to exercise his influence and skill for the benefit of the society within which he and his organisation operate.

National Union of Journalists Code of Conduct

1. A journalist has a duty to maintain the highest professional and ethical standards.

2. A journalist shall at all times defend the principles of the freedom of the Press and other media in relation to the collection of information and the expression of comment and criticism. He/she shall strive to eliminate distortion, news suppression and censorship.

3. A journalist shall strive to ensure that the information he/she disseminates is fair and accurate, avoid the expression of comment and conjecture as established fact and falsification by distortion, selection or misrepresentation.

4. A journalist shall rectify promptly any harmful inaccuracies, ensure that corrections and apologies receive due prominence and afford the right of reply to persons criticised when the issue is of sufficient importance.

5. A journalist shall obtain information, photographs and illustration only by straightforward means. The use of other means can be justified only by overriding considerations of the public interest. The journalist is entitled to exercise a personal conscientious objection to the use of such means.

6. Subject to justification by overriding considerations of the public interest, a journalist shall do nothing which entails intrusion into private grief and distress.

7. A journalist shall protect confidential sources of information.

8. A journalist shall not accept bribes nor shall he/she allow other inducements to influence the performance of his/her professional duties.

9. A journalist shall not lend himself/herself to the distortion or suppression of the truth because of advertising or other considerations.

10. A journalist shall only mention a person's race, colour, creed, disability, illegitimacy, marital status (or lack of it), age, gender, sexual orientation if this information is strictly relevant. A journalist shall neither originate nor process material which encourages discrimination on any of the above-mentioned grounds.

11. A journalist shall not take private advantage of information gained in the course of his/her duties, before the information is public knowledge.

12. A journalist shall not by way of statement, voice or appearance endorse by advertisement any commercial product or device save for the promotion of his/her own work or of the medium by which he/she is employed.

IABC Code of Ethics

The IABC (International Association of Business Communicators) Code of Ethics has been developed to provide IABC members and other communication professionals with guidelines of professional behaviour and standards of ethical practice. The Code will be reviewed and revised as necessary by the Ethics Committee and the Executive Board.

Any IABC member who wishes advice and guidance regarding its interpretation and/or application may write to or phone IABC headquarters. Questions will be routed to the Executive Board member responsible for the Code.

Communication and information dissemination

1. Communication professionals will uphold the credibility and dignity of their profession by encouraging the practice of honest, candid and timely communication.

    The highest standards of professionalism will be upheld in all communication. Communicators should encourage frequent communication and messages that are honest in their content, candid, accurate and appropriate to the needs of the organisation and its audiences.

2. Professional communicators will not use any information that has been generated or appropriately acquired by a business for another business without permission. Further, communicators should attempt to identify the source of information to be used.

    When one is changing employers, information developed at the previous position will not be used without permission from that employer. Acts of plagiarism and copyright infringement are illegal acts; material in the public domain should have its source attributed, if possible. If an organisation grants permission to use its information and requests public acknowledgement, it will be made in a place appropriate to the material used. The material will be used only for the purpose for which permission was granted.

Standards of conduct

3. Communication professionals will abide by the spirit and letter of all laws and regulations governing their professional activities.

    All international, national and local laws and regulations must be observed, with particular attention to those pertaining to communication, such as copyright law. Industry and organisational regulations will also be observed.

4. Communication professionals will not condone any illegal or unethical act related to their professional activity, their organisation and its business or the public environment in which it operates.

It is the personal responsibility of professional communicators to act honestly, fairly and with integrity at all times in all professional activities. Looking the other way while others act illegally tacitly condones such acts whether or not the communicator has committed them. The communicator should speak with the individual involved, his or her supervisor or appropriate authorities – depending on the context of the situation and one's own ethical judgement.

Confidentiality/disclosure

5. Communication professionals will respect the confidentiality and right to privacy of all individuals, employers, clients and customers.

Communicators must determine the ethical balance between right to privacy and need to know. Unless this situation involves illegal or grossly unethical acts, confidences should be maintained. If there is a conflict between right to privacy and need to know, a communicator should first talk with the source and negotiate the need for the information to be communicated.

6. Communication professionals will not use any confidential information gained as a result of professional activity for personal benefit or for that of others.

Confidential information can be used to give inside advantage to stock transactions, gain favours from outsiders, assist a competing company for whom one is going to work, assist companies in developing a marketing advantage, achieve a publishing advantage or otherwise act to the detriment of an organisation. Such information must remain confidential during and after one's employment period.

Professionalism

7. Communication professionals should uphold IABC's standards for ethical conduct in all professional activity, and should use IABC and its designation of accreditation (ABC) only for purposes that are

authorised and fairly represent the organisation and its professional standards.

IABC recognises the need for professional integrity within any organisation, including the association. Members should acknowledge that their actions reflect on themselves, their organisations and their profession.

Appendix III

QUALITY ASSURANCE

The quality of goods and services sold is an important component of good corporate citizenship. Britain leads the world in quality assurance; and the British Standards Institution philosophy and system have been taken up not only by the most successful British firms, but also internationally, forming the bases for the International Standards Organisation's own series of standards. All goods and services can benefit; from buildings and machinery to furnishings, chemicals, foods, guided weapons and computer software, and from opera and scientific research to package holidays and health services, for example.

Quality assurance includes responsibilities of the manufacturer or supplier of a product or service ('quality management' and 'quality control'), and also those of the purchaser or customer, and of any regulatory or certification body as well. 150 standards documents are published in several different languages, and are applied in many countries; exact definitions of terminology are published in English, French and Russian. There are basic standards concerning quality assurance, reliability of 'constructed or manufactured products, systems, equipments and components', definitive standards for quality, measurement and calibration systems; and advice on all the components of controlling quality-related costs. The whole concept of quality is catered for, from thought-through design and production (where relevant) to realization. Charts, diagrams and descriptions help the user navigate through the complex and interlinked issues.

Attitude of mind is of major importance – from top to bottom of any organisation. 'Best means' for quality does not mean 'most expensive', and certainly not 'wasteful'; and 'most effective' does not mean 'easiest' or 'quickest' but 'most efficient and most satisfactory'. Similarly, prevention of future faults is much better than having to discover, and then cure, them. Finally, reliability, too, can be quantified especially in its effect on reducing life-cycle costs of goods and services. The British Standard on reliability is as long as those on all the other components of quality assurance combined.

This is an important advance in professional and industrial thinking and practice for all services, supplies and products. To apply quality assurance many specialisms are required, which takes time and effort. But all suppliers can benefit themselves and their customers by understanding the dangers of not instituting quality assurance, and the considerable advantages of developing within its philosophy and realization.

Appendix IV

THE CLUB OF ROME – AN ORGANISATION OF SPECIAL SIGNIFICANCE

Secrétariat Général, 34 avenue l'Eylau, 75116 Paris, France; British Association for the Club of Rome, The Court House, Bisley, Stroud, Glos GL6 7AA.

The Club of Rome studies components and issues of citizenship – global, regional, national, even personal and corporate – and has been called an 'invisible university' with concern for humanity and the future of the world. It is a non-governmental group of a hundred individuals worldwide convinced of the urgent need for a deeper understanding of the rapid evolution of world society. Many problems facing mankind are so complex and interrelated that traditional institutions find them difficult to comprehend and control. Population growth, increasing pollution, Third World debt, developing terrorism and bourgeoning communications are some examples of problems: while the recently reduced tension between superpowers, successful demonstrations of 'people power', and increasing environmental awareness, for instance, give reasons for hope.

Founded in 1968 by Aurelio Peccei, an Italian industrial leader, and by Alexander King, a Scottish scientist, its members come from 50 countries on five continents – socialist republics and monarchies, agriculture-based economies and industrialised countries, old-established nations and new ones. Its members are distinguished engineers, scientists, economists, sociologists, philosophers, administrators, high officials and religious, business, academic and industrial leaders, but not politicians in office.

The members of the Club of Rome are committed to working together, respecting each others' convictions and holding joint discussions despite their divergent opinions. The following original approaches still serve as the bases for the thinking and action of members:

- Adopting a global approach to the vast and complex problems of the world in which interdependence among nations on a finite earth is becoming increasingly close.

190

- Seeking a deeper understanding of the interactions within the tangle of current and developing problems – political, economic, social, industrial, cultural, psychological, technological, environmental – for which the Club of Rome coined the phrase 'the world problematique'.
- Focusing on long-term perspectives, options and policies that will determine the lot of future generations. By contrast, governments and institutions, all too often locked into existing structures and administrations and in many cases necessarily responding mainly to the immediate concerns of insufficiently informed constituencies, tend to make short-term issues their priorities.

Expert organisations are commissioned to carry out the researches so as to extend understanding of chosen topics. There are no 'Club of Rome Reports', but rather 'Reports *to* (or *for*) the Club of Rome', published on the decision of the Executive Committee without necessarily implying all the members' agreement in their purport. The aim is to stimulate thinking and discussion, rather than to present actual plans or forecasts.

The first report to the Club of Rome, *The Limits to Growth*, sold some 10 million in 37 languages and triggered off a heated debate which is still going on. The Report was even mistakenly associated with the zero-growth concept formulated by Sicco Mansholt. However, the Club of Rome has pursued its research within the framework of the world problematique on a great variety of topics: reports have been published on the need for a new world order, the reorientation of educational systems, the social impact of new technologies, Third World problems, and so on.

The implications of these reports have been widely debated during international conferences and seminars held all over the world: in Algiers, Berlin, Berne, Bogota, Budapest, Canberra, Caracas, Hanover, Helsinki, Kuwait, Mexico City, Moscow, New York, Paris, Philadelphia, Rio de Janeiro, Santander, Seoul, Tokyo, Toronto, Warsaw and Yaoundé, for example.

For further effectiveness, the Club of Rome also helped create a number of specialised organisations such as the Foundation for International Training (Don Mills, Canada) or the International Federation of Institutes for Advanced Studies.

It has also arranged studies at the request of international agencies such as Unesco (for example on the role of ethical values in education) and co-operated with many universities.

The Club of Rome tries to accept invitations from groups of business interests, bankers, students, or government leaders in various parts of the world, with the object of organising discussions with them on the perspectives opened up by the responses to the great questions of our times.

The Club of Rome approach can be summed up in a formula: think globally, act locally. For this reason national associations for the Club of Rome have been founded in Argentina, Australia, Austria, Canada, Columbia, Egypt, Finland, France, Great Britain, Japan, Morocco, the Netherlands, New Zealand, Poland, Turkey, the United States, USSR, Venezuela and West Germany, with a three-point mission defined by a charter: to inform the Club of Rome of the evolution of problems in their countries and regions; to serve as relays for Club of Rome ideas, debates and actions; and to take initiatives and launch projects with the object of making progress in the solutions to local problems and contributing to studies undertaken by the Club of Rome.

The aim of the Club of Rome is not merely to be a research and study organisation. It considers that it has to act, particularly by sharing the results of its work with men and women of decision and power, stimulating world-wide discussions (which is rarely possible within official structures) and suggesting solutions and strategies. To this effect, the Club of Rome maintains contacts with many political figures and has organised several meetings with heads of state and government.

At the same time, one of the Club of Rome's concerns is to help people to a better grasp of the issues at stake for the future, and therefore to inform the general public of the changes that are constantly occurring in the world, often unknown to them. Indeed, the conviction is that men and women need not remain passive and isolated as spectators of the great world phenomena, the consequences of which they must only enjoy or suffer. Furthermore, the Club of Rome believes that for the world problematique, only the participation of all individuals, non-governmental organisations, firms and official institutions joined in a common effort, will enable the elaboration of the complex set of interactive solutions for which it proposes the term 'world resolutique'.

The Club of Rome chose for the theme of their 20th Anniversary Conference in Paris in 1988, 'The Great Transition – Reasons to Live and Hope in a New Global Society'; the theme for their 1989 Conference in Hanover was 'Global Industrialisation – Vision or Nightmare?'. Recommendations included combining competition with co-operation; encouraging quality in growth and reducing disparities between living standards; deriving global strategies for both industrialisation and environmental improvement; and developing both education and dialogue on the issues involved. Among other positive measures the Club of Rome called for a North–South conference on environmental imperatives; a Co-operation Global Development Round of industrial leaders, bankers and governments of five continents; and a UN Environmental Security Council parallel to the existing Security Council on military matters. These recommendations are being taken up at the highest level in the United Nations.

Appendix V

USEFUL ORGANISATIONS AND PUBLICATIONS

Organisations

> The Advertising Association
> Abford House
> 15 Wilton Road
> London
> SW1V 1NJ
> Sara Bayley (Public Affairs Executive)

The Advertising Association is a federation of 29 trade associations and professional bodies representing advertisers, agencies, the media and support services. It is the lobbying of organisation for the UK advertising industry on British and European legislative proposals and other issues of common concern, at both national and international levels, and as such campaigns actively to maintain the freedom to advertise and to improve public attitudes to advertising. It publishes UK and European statistics on advertising expenditure, instigates research on advertising issues, and organises seminars and courses for people in the communications business. Its Information Centre is one of the country's leading sources of advertising and associated subjects.

> Association for Business Sponsorship of the Arts (ABSA)
> Nutmeg House
> 60 Gainsford Street
> London
> SE1 2NY

ABSA is an independent national organisation, launched in 1976, which aims to promote and facilitate the principles and practice of arts sponsorship in the United Kingdom. Annual arts sponsorship has grown since ABSA's formation in 1976 from £600,000 to over £30 million. ABSA now has over 240 business members and four offices in London, Edinburgh, Belfast and Cardiff.

A business joining ABSA can expect the following:

- Advice on a sponsorship programme.
- Access to the register of sponsorship opportunities.
- Research on the best package to achieve sponsorship objectives.
- Invitations to gala evenings, seminars, private views, and the ABSA Daily Telegraph Awards ceremony.
- Introductions to other sponsors and the arts.
- Receipt of ABSA publications.
- Lobbying on behalf of the business community for better media credits and tax reform.

In addition to these functions, ABSA administers the government's Business Sponsorship Incentive Scheme, which acts as an incentive to businesses to sponsor the arts for the first time or to increase their budget. ABSA also runs a new initiative, Business in the Arts, which aims to improve the quality of arts management with the involvement of the business sector.

Association of Exhibition Organisers Ltd (AEO)
1 Totteridge Avenue
High Wycombe
Bucks
HP13 6XG
A. Whittle (Administration Director)

Formed in 1920, the Association became a limited company in 1969 and has developed steadily since. With its substantial membership, it has the reputation of being a leading force in the exhibition industry. Resources have been put into promoting the industry and the interests of members. It organises a variety of functions for members to exchange views and ideas, and provides a meeting forum. Links have been forged with both Westminster and Whitehall, to focus on the importance of the exhibition industry to the economy.

Association of Free Newspapers (AFN)
27 Brunswick Square
Gloucester
GL1 1UN
John Gerrie (Executive Director)

The main activities of the AFN are directed to the development of awareness of the free distribution targeted medium as an effective advertising vehicle. It organises an annual conference, provides a monthly newspaper and maintains a database to provide a media planning service for agencies. Services for members include a group libel scheme, regular newsletters and a 'help-line' for legal, employment and personnel, health and safety, and tax investigation advice.

> Association of Independent Radio Contractors Ltd (AIRC)
> Regina House
> 259–69 Old Marylebone Road
> London
> NW1 5RA
> Brian West (Director)

All companies holding franchises awarded by the IBA are members of the AIRC. It provides a forum for the companies and represents their views to the government, the IBA, trade unions and copyright bodies. It co-ordinates industry programming initiatives, such as the Network Chart Show. AIRC's subsidiary, the Radio Marketing Bureau, promotes radio to advertisers and agencies and co-ordinates network advertising activity.

> Audit Bureau of Circulations Ltd (ABC)
> 13 Wimpole Street
> London
> W1M 7AB
> John Holmes (Director)

With a tripartite membership of advertisers, agencies and publishers, ABC is responsible for the certification of circulation of newspapers, consumer and business publications exhibition data provided by independent professional auditors using standard audit procedures. These are accepted by space buyers as authentic. Verified Free Distribution Ltd, at same address, is a wholly-owned subsidiary providing a similar service for free publications which cannot be certified under ABC rules which require each copy to be separately wrapped and addressed.

> British Association for the Advancement of Science
> Fortress House
> 23 Savile Row
> London
> W1X 1AB

The British Association for the Advancement of Science was founded in 1831. Its aims are to enhance public understanding and awareness of science and technology; and to increase public support for science and technology. It can pursue these aims by working with people to stimulate their enthusiasm for science and technology; and promoting links between scientists and others in industry and commerce, the media, Parliament and the general public.

> The British Association of Industrial Editors (BAIE)
> 3 Locks Yard
> High Street
> Sevenoaks
> Kent
> TN13 1LT
> Cecil Pedersen (Chief Executive)

The BAIE is the professional association for (internal) corporate communications. Its main services include the annual Communicator of the Year award, Editing for Industry Awards, education and training, an annual study conference, and publications including the *Editor's Handbook* (a major loose/internal corporate communications using various media: newspapers, magazines, videos, annual reports, etc.).

Membership of BAIE is open to all individuals, whether directors, managers, editors or assistants engaged in the management, editing or production of corporate communications media. BAIE defines internal corporate communications to include all media produced as a means of communication between an organisation and its shareholders, customers, suppliers, employees, etc.

> British Overseas Trade Board (BOTB)
> Marketing and Briefing Unit
> 1–19 Victoria Street
> London
> SW1H 0ET
> Jean Cleary

The BOTB guides and directs the export promotion services of the Department of Trade and Industry. Its services provide a wide range of assistance to existing and potential exporters in both manufacturing and service industries. Members are mainly businessmen with practical knowledge of exporting. In addition to the London headquarters, there are ten regional offices throughout the United Kingdom.

British Printing Industries Federation
11 Bedford Row
London
WC1R 4DX
Marion Young (Head of Public Relations)

The BPIF has a technical database on over 3,000 member companies and can provide names and addresses of suppliers in specific areas. It also provides guidance on a host of subjects, such as training and legislation, and economic data.

Business in the Community
227a City Road
London
EC1V 1LX
Stephen O'Brien (Chief Executive)

BiC is an association of major UK businesses committed to working in partnership with each other, with central and local government, voluntary organisations and trade unions to promote corporate social responsibility and revitalise economic life in local communities. BiC does this by working with its members and others to take action which demonstrates the creative role that business can play in economic revitalisation and enterprise, mainly through pioneering projects which can be replicated on a wider basis, and through forms of business support which can become part of mainstream business practice.

In carrying out these activities BiC is politically non-aligned and aims to be professional, demonstrate good value for money from resources subscribed by members, pursue priorities relevant to mainstream business practice and collaborate as far as possible with other bodies which share BiC's goals.

The Business Network
18 Well Walk
Hampstead
London
NW3 1LD
Marilyn Rose (Administration)

The Business Network links business people and others interested in transforming business so that it embodies a vision of the wholeness of life for the planet and for the human spirit. It informs, supports and encourages those who seek to harmonise these aspects in their personal and business lives, operating a programme of regular activities, including events and communications.

> The Cavity Foam Bureau
> PO Box 79, Oldbury, Warley,
> West Midlands
> B69 4PW
> Ernest Hodgson (Administration)

The Association represents the raw materials manufacturers, systems designers and insulation contractors who are members of the British Standards Institution Registered Firms Scheme for the installation of UF foam cavity wall insulation. As such the Association is one of many sector trade associations where members have joined together to help promote higher standards of practice and information for their industry.

> Chartered Institute of Marketing (CIM)
> Moor Hall
> Cookham
> Maidenhead
> Berks
> SL6 9QH
> Joanna Barrett (Marketing Executive)

Founded in 1911, the CIM is the largest marketing management organisation in Europe. Its primary function is to increase the level of awareness and understanding of marketing as a vital factor in business success and to stimulate enhanced marketing performance throughout commerce and industry in the United Kingdom. It undertakes research into business and is involved with the government and other influential bodies in bringing the benefits of marketing excellence to the attention of industry and commerce via conferences, political lobbying, the media and the membership itself. Membership is over 22,000 (with 20,000 students throughout the world).

> Communication, Advertising and Marketing
> Education Foundation Ltd (CAM Foundation)
> Abford House
> 15 Wilton Road
> London
> SW1V 1NJ
> Dr Steve Carter (Chairman, Examinations Board)

The examining body for vocational qualifications in the different functions of communication, set up by 20 institutes and associations which control the nature of each syllabus and the standard of the examinations. CAM qualifications are at two levels – Part I is the Certificate and Part II the Diploma. The entry requirements for the Certificates are equivalent to those for university entrance. Since the Certificate covers the whole area of the UK communication business it is literally an 'industry induction'. The CAM examinations at Diploma level are designed for those who wish to specialise in their chosen career.

> Consumers' Association
> 2 Marylebone Road
> London
> NW1 4DX

The Consumers' Association has over a million members, and publishes *Which?* and many useful books. It also campaigns on special and selected issues, of interest to consumers.

> Department of Trade and Industry (DTI)
> 1–19 Victoria Street
> London
> SW1H 0ET

In providing its range of services for exporters, the DTI works through the British Overseas Trade Board (q.v.). The Board's members come mainly from industry and commerce, bringing practical experience of exporting and overseas markets.

DTI's Export Initiative provides help, advice and support to companies of all sizes. It aims to encourage potential exporters to think seriously about selling overseas and existing exporters to sell more.

The first point of contact for the Export Initiative is the nearest DTI Regional Office, Scottish Office, Welsh Office or the Industrial Development Board in Northern Ireland.

DTI North East	DTI South West
(091) 232 4722	(0272) 272666
DTI North West	DTI South East
(061) 236 2171	(071)215 5000
DTI Yorkshire and Humberside	Scotland
(0532) 443171	(041) 248 2855
DTI East Midlands	Wales
(0602)506181	(0222) 825097
DTI West Midlands	Northern Ireland
(021)631 6181	(0232) 233233

Design Council
28 Haymarket
London
SW1Y 4SU
Janet Hall (Publicity Officer)

The Design Council is a government-funded organisation which encourages and promotes the improvement of design in the products of British industry. It provides advice to companies on the solution of design problems through the Design Advisory Service and Support for Design Scheme; produces the *Design Directory*, a comprehensive list and recommendation service for design skills in Britain; and publishes books and magazines, including *Design* and *Engineering*.

DESTECH
37 Cadogan Street
London
SW3 2PR
Brian Locke (Hon. Secretary)

The Association for Design and Technology Education (DESTECH), inaugurated in 1984 and more recently registered as a charity, works to develop the design engineering, industrial and scientific content of education at all levels, in the expectation that this must lead to a balanced understanding of life in the round. It has already helped bring technology into the core curriculum, and its achievements, without grant aid and in only five years, are considerable.

Direct Mail Producers' Association (DMPA)
34 Grand Avenue
London
N10 3BP
Mark Elwes (Executive Director)

The DMPA is the trade association for agencies engaged in direct mail activities on behalf of their clients. It has currently over 120 member companies. It can provide advice to advertisers who are contemplating the use of direct mail or who are seeking specialist support. It handles some 3,000 enquiries a year.

Friends of the Earth Ltd
26–28 Underwood Street
London
N1 7TQ
Jonathon Porritt (Director)

Friends of the Earth is one of the leading environmental lobbying and pressure groups in the UK. It blows the whistle on those who destroy the environment and puts pressure on those who have the power to protect it. It has a network of more than 270 groups across the UK; internationally, it is now represented in more than 35 countries.

> Incorporated Society of British Advertisers Ltd (ISBA)
> 44 Hertford Street
> London
> WiY 8AE
> Kenneth Miles (Director)

ISBA is the only organisation which exclusively represents the interests and needs of 'client companies' for whom advertising is an important element in their marketing plans. Its membership includes most leading companies, many being international groups based outside Britain. ISBA priorities include contact with all media owners and their associations, with government and official bodies such as the Independent Broadcasting Authority (q.v.), Office of Fair Trading (q.v.), and the Monopolies and Mergers Commission, as well as international bodies such as the European Commission, Council of Europe and International Chamber of Commerce.

ISBA strongly supports Codes of Practice in advertising and promotional activities, and frequently supplies people to participate in, or lead, the key committees for such Codes. Advice and guidelines on many areas of business practice are frequently given to companies.

> Independent Broadcasting Authority (IBA)
> 70 Brompton Road
> London
> SW3 1EY
> Miss S. M. Fewell (Senior Information Assistant)

Independent television (ITV and Channel 4) regularly attracts the greater share of the available viewing audience and its programmes have also earned an enviable reputation overseas. Together with independent local radio, these services are completely self-supporting, deriving their income from the sale of spot advertising time. The IBA is the public body responsible for ensuring that programmes and schedules are in accordance with the provisions of the Broadcasting Act 1981.

Independent Television Association
Knighton House
56 Mortimer Street
London
WiN 8AN
D. Shaw (Director)

This is the central body serving the needs of the 16 independent television contractors currently operating in the United Kingdom. It undertakes on behalf of its members those activities which need to be handled or co-ordinated centrally. Generally matters are dealt with by the Central Secretariat, and a number of standing committees exist to deal with specific areas such as programming, marketing, public relations and industrial relations.

The Industrial Society
Robert Hyde House
48 Bryanston Square
London
WiH 7LN
Jean Balcombe (Head of Information Services)

The Industrial Society works to develop the full talents and potential of people at work and those seeking work, and to increase employee involvement and personal fulfilment through work. It promotes equal opportunities at work and in access to employment, training and development. Its aim is to maximise the contribution that people working in organisations of all kinds can make to UK prosperity and to the well-being of the community. The Society concentrates on eight main areas:

- Encouraging high performance and commitment through effective leadership.
- Communicating and achieving business objectives.
- Developing the full talents and potential of people at work.
- Developing productive employee relations.
- Achieving equal opportunity.
- Widening horizons for young people.
- Improving employment prospects for people seeking work.
- Helping organisations overseas, particularly in developing countries, gain the management and leadership skills necessary to develop their economies.

The Institute of Business Ethics
12 Palace Street
London
SW1E 5JA
Stanley Klaer (Director)

The Institute of Business Ethics has been founded to provide a forum for study, research and opinion formation in the field of business ethics. Its task includes emphasising the positive aspects of wealth creation and promoting the ethical principles which should underlie a sound business environment in a free society.

Institute of Directors
116 Pall Mall
London
SW1Y 5ED
Gordon Leak (Public Relations Director)

Founded in 1903, this is the largest representative business organisation committed to the defence and promotion of free enterprise. It aims to provide an effective voice to represent the interests of its members and to bring the experience of the business leader to bear on the conduct of public affairs. Its members are directors of public and private companies, partners and professional men and women.

The Institute of Energy
18 Devonshire Street
London
W1N 2AU
Colin Rigg (Secretary)

The Institute of Energy was founded in 1927 and incorporated by Royal Charter in 1946. Its aims are 'to promote the effective provision, conversion, transmission and utilisation of energy in all its forms, with due regard to the prudent use of resources and the protection of the environment'. The Institute of Energy is the learned society for engineers, scientists and technologists actively engaged in the production, conversion, distribution and use of energy in all forms. Through regular technical meetings and conferences, and through the publications *Energy World*, *The Journal*, *Energy World Yearbook* and *Fuel & Energy Abstracts*, members keep abreast of technical, economic and political developments on the energy scene.

Institute of Export
Export House
64 Clifton Street
London
EC2A 4HB
M. L Sansom (Director, International Services)

This professional association for managers and companies engaged in overseas trade was incorporated in 1935. It seeks to set and raise the standards of export practice and management through formal and informal education and the exchange of ideas and information between members. It publishes a journal (ten issues per year), operates a staff bureau and export specialists' service, represents members' views to the government and provides an information service.

Institute of Practitioners in Advertising (IPA)
44 Belgrave Square
London
SW1X 8QS
Nick Phillips (Director-General)

The IPA is the professional and trade organisation for UK advertising agencies. It represents the collective view of agencies, and the people who work in them, in discussions and negotiations with government departments, the media, and industry and consumer organisations. It also makes an important contribution to the effective operation of advertising agencies through its advisory, training and information services. It has well over 1,400 personal members, and 250 member agencies who between them handle over 80 per cent of all advertising placed by UK agencies.

Institute of Public Relations (IPR)
The Old Trading House
15 Northborough
London
EC1V oPR
J. B. Lavelle (Executive Director)

The IPR represents and regulates professional PR practitioners in the United Kingdom. It was founded in 1948 and is by far the largest organisation of its kind in Europe. Its concern is to maintain and raise the standard of professional practice, so ensuring that public relations practice deserves and achieves status, recognition and understanding.

Institute of Trading Standards Administration
4/5 Hadleigh Business Centre
351 London Road
Hadleigh
Essex SS7 2BT

This is the professional body for trading standards officers, who investigate complaints and enforce laws relating to false or misleading descriptions or prices, inaccurate weights and measures, and some aspects of the safety of goods and of consumer credit, as well as providing help and advice both to traders and consumers.

International Association of Business Communicators (IABC)
Eagle House
110 Jermyn Street
London
SW1Y 6HA
Marian Hawkins

The IABC is an American-based organisation for over 10,000 employee relations and public affairs managers, writers, audio-visual specialists, consultants and others who are involved or interested in organisational communication. The UK branch was established in 1979 and runs workshops, seminars and social events. The IABC publishes an international monthly magazine and the UK branch publishes its own newsletter. An annual convention is held. The IABC has published a code of business ethics.

International Public Relations Association (IPRA)
Case Postale 126
CH-1211 Geneva 20
Switzerland
Anthony J. Murdoch (Secretary-General)

Founded in 1955, IPRA is a professional organisation, dedicated to high standards of practice and mutual understanding between groups, organisations and nations.

Market Research Society (MRS)
175 Oxford Street
London
W1R 1TA
Roger Sargood (Acting Director-General)

MRS is the professional body for market research practitioners. It administers the Diploma in Market Research (the only professional qualification solely concerned with market research) and has an extensive programme of other training courses, which are open to non-members. The society produces a range of publications dealing with market research. It was established in 1946 and has 6,500 members.

National Association of Citizens Advice Bureaux
Myddelton House
115–23 Pentonville Road
London
N1 9LZ

Over 1,000 outlets throughout the United Kingdom (listed in Phone Books) provide the consumer with wide-ranging information, advice and assistance.

National Consumer Council
20 Grosvenor Gardens
London
SW1W 0DH

The National Consumer Council is an independent organisation with government funding. Its job is to further and safeguard the interests of consumers and to speak up for them to public utilities, business, industry, the professions and government, both central and local.

Office of Fair Trading (OFT)
Field House
Breams Buildings
London
EC4 1PR

The OFT is concerned with the conduct of trade and industry in the United Kingdom, whether large or small. It deals with consumer credit monopolies and mergers as well as with restrictive practices. The office also publishes useful consumer advice and literature.

Public Relations Consultants Association
Premier House
10 Greycoat Place
London
SW1P 1SB
C. G. Thompson (Director)

Formed in 1968, the Public Relations Consultants Association represents over 80 per cent of consultancies in terms of fee income. Members have to conform to a strict code of practice. The Association represents members in dealings with the government, commercial bodies and education and training bodies. It also sponsors awards for outstanding consultancy and seminars, and encourages the development of business through management documents. It provides potential clients with a simple selection system through a computer matrix and is always available to give advice.

> The Royal Society for the Encouragement of Arts Manufacturers
> & Commerce
> 8 John Adam Street
> London
> WC2N 6EZ
> Christopher Lucas (Secretary and Chief Executive)

The RSA has always seen the arts as an essential component in the life of a civilised nation. Its commitment to the arts is a natural complement to its commitment to manufacturers and commerce. It is committed to the encouragement of manufactures and commerce because it believes these activities to be central to the prosperity and thus the well-being of the nation. Design makes a vital contribution to successful industrial production. In encouraging high standards in design, the RSA marries two of its long-standing interests: the expression of human potential through creativity and the encouragement of manufacturers and commerce.

The RSA's concern for education reflects its belief that in a successful society, individuals are enabled to maximise their talents in a way which not only leads to self-fulfilment but also contributes to that society's needs and purposes and to social cohesion and prosperity.

The RSA has consistently believed that we all have a responsibility to protect and enhance the environment, whether natural or man-made, in the interests not only of our own health and well-being but also of future generations.

> Society of Consumer Affairs Professionals in Business (SOCAP)
> London House
> 53–54 Haymarket
> London
> SW1Y 4RP

SOCAP is a professional organisation of individuals whose purpose is to foster and maintain the integrity of business in dealings with consumers, encourage and promote effective communications and understanding between business, government and consumers, and to define and advance the consumer affairs profession. It was founded in 1973 in the United States, with the UK branch being founded in 1985. SOCAP UK has just over 100 member companies from various sectors – retailers, manufacturers, the motor trade, travel, leisure and financial institutions, as well as specialist consumer affairs consultancies.

The Soil Association
86 Colston Street
Bristol
BS1 5BB
Sue Stolton (Publicity)

The Soil Association was established as a charity in 1946 to define the standards of organic production. Its inspectors visit organic producers, allowing those whose methods come up to its standards to sell their produce using its coveted symbol of quality. It works with three sister organisations (British Organic Farmers, the Organic Growers Association, and the Elm Farm Research Centre) to encourage and assist growers wishing to produce real organic food. It also researches organic issues and publishes its findings, as well as providing expert advice to governments in Britain and overseas and fighting hard for environmental protection. It has an active membership, a magazine and over 40 local groups.

The Watt Committee on Energy
Savoy Hill House
Savoy Hill
London
WC2R 0BU
Graham Mordue (Secretary)

The Watt Committee on Energy is an independent voluntary body representing some 60 British professional institutions and acts as a forum for discussion of all aspects of energy and related technologies.

The Committee's declared objectives are to promote and assist energy research and development, disseminate knowledge, promote the formation of informed opinion, and encourage the constructive analysis of energy questions as an aid to strategic planning for the benefit of all.

Wider Share Ownership Council
Juxon House
94 St Paul's Churchyard
London
EC4M 8EH
E. W. I. Palamountain (Chairman)

This influential organisation lobbies for wider recognition of the benefits of share ownership, including employee share ownership plans, and the rights of shareholders.

Publications

Magazines

Achievement
World Trade Magazine Ltd
World Trade House
145 High Street
Sevenoaks
Kent TN13 1XL
(0732) 458144

A magazine devoted to reporting on major international capital projects.

Broadcast
100 Avenue Road
Swiss Cottage
London
NW3 3TP
(071) 935 6611

Important weekly for the broadcasting industry.

Conference Britain
Bofoers Publishing Limited
Bofoers House
2 Bentinck Court
Bentinck Road
West Drayton
Middlesex UB7 7RQ
(0895) 431431/422414

The leading UK magazine for organisers of conferences, exhibitions, meetings and incentive travel.

Design
The Design Council
28 Haymarket
London
SW1Y 4SU
(071) 839 8000

Informs managers and designers about industrial design.

Director
The Director Publications Ltd
Mountbarrow House
6–20 Elizabeth Street
London
SW1W 9RB
(071) 730 6060

Leading monthly magazine for chief executives, directors and business men and women.

Marketing
22 Lancaster Gate
London
W2 3LY1
(071) 402 4200

Important weekly for the marketing industry.

New Consumer
52 Elswick Road
Newcastle Upon Tyne
NE4 6JH
(091) 272 1148

This magazine describes its purpose as 'to provide people with information and practical strategies for integrating their economic choices with their values and lifestyles'.

UK Press Gazette
Mitre House
44 Fleet Street
(Entrance Metre Court)
London
EC4Y 1BS
(071) 583 6463

Influential publication read in the main by journalists.

Books

Advertiser's Annual
Thomas Skinner Directories
Windsor Court
East Grinstead
West Sussex RH9 1XE
(0342) 26972

British Rate and Data (BRAD)
1a Chalk Lane
Cockfosters
London
(081) 441 6644

Benn's Media Directory
Benn's Business Information Services Ltd
PO Box 20
Sovereign Way
Tonbridge
Kent TN9 1RQ
(0732) 362666

Hollis Press & Public Relations Annual
Contact House
Lower Hampton Road
Sunbury-on-Thames
Middlesex TW16 5HG
(0932) 784781

Public Relations Year Book
PRCA
Premier House
10 Greycoat Place
London
SW1P 1SB
(071) 222 8866

Bibliography

ABSA/WH Smith
Sponsorship Manual. (Available ABSA, see Appendix V.)
Anthony, W. P.
The Social Responsibility of Business. Morristown, NJ: D. H. Mark
Publication of General Learning Press, 1973.
Arthur Andersen
Tax Guide to Arts Sponsorship. (Available ABSA, see Appendix V.)
Barnham, K. and Rassam, C.
Shaping the Corporate Future. London: Unwin Hyman, 1989.
Baumhart, R. S. J.
Ethics in Business. New York: Holt, Rinehart & Winston, 1968.
Behrman, J. N.
Discourses on Ethics and Business. Cambridge, Mass.: Oelgeschlager,
Gunn & Hair, 1981.
Blanchard, K. and Peale, N. V.
The Power of Ethical Management. London: Heinemann Kingswood,
1988.
Bowie, N.
Business Ethics. Englewood Cliffs, NJ: Prentice Hall, 1982.
Bowman, P.
Handbook of Financial and Public Relations. Oxford: Heinemann,
1989.
Buzzacott,
Charities and Business: A partnership of interest. London: Buzzacott &
Co, 1989.
Carmichael, S. and Drummond, J.
Good Business: A guide to corporate responsibility and business ethics.
London: Business Books Ltd, 1989.

CBI
Initiatives Beyond Charity. Report of the CBI Task Force on Business and Urban Regeneration, London, 1988.
Cook, R. A. and Ryan, L. V.
'The relevance of ethics to management education'. *Journal of Management Development,* 7, 2, 28–32.
Deal, T. and Kennedy, A.
Corporate Cultures. Reading Mass.: Addison-Wesley, 1982.
De George *et al* (eds)
Ethics, Free Enterprise and Public Policy: Original essays on moral issues in business. New York: Oxford University Press, 1978.
Department of the Environment
Environment In Trust. London: HMSO, 1989.
Elkington J. and Hailes, J.
The Green Consumer Guide. Victor Gollancz Ltd, 1988.
Fernstrom, M. M.
Corporate Public Responsibility And The Role Of Advertising. American Advertising Federation Second District Conference, New York: American Express Company, 1985.
Fernstrom, M. M.
Financial Institutions And The Public Interest: Forging joint ventures. American Express Company, 1989.
Fink, S.
Crisis Management, Planning For The Inevitable. AMACOM, New York, 1986.
Gerrett, T. M.
Business Ethics. Englewood Cliffs, NJ: Prentice Hall, 1966.
Goyder, G.
The Just Enterprise. London: André Deutsch, 1987.
Harvard Business Review
Ethics for Executive Series. Cambridge, Mass: President and Fellows of Harvard College, 1955.
Harvey-Jones, J.
Making It Happen: Reflections on leadership. London: William Collins, 1988.
Hoffman, W. M., and Wyly, T. J. (eds)
The Work Ethic in Business. Proceedings of the Cluid National Conference on Business Ethics, Cambridge, Mass.: Oelgeschlager Gunn & Hair, 1979.
Irvine, S. and Ponton, A.
A Green Manifesto. London: Macdonald Optima, 1988.

Ivens, M. (ed.)
Industry and Values. London: Harrap, 1970.
Jennings, M. and Churchill, D.
Getting the Message Across: A guide to directing corporate communications. Cambridge: Director Books, 1988.
Kinsman, F.
Tomorrow's Workplace: The manager's guide to teleworking. London: Customer Communications Unit of British Telecommunications plc, 1989.
Mirams, P.
Great Britain, The Conservation of Our Heritage. London: Torrobay Ltd, 1989
Newsom, D.
Crisis Categories And Constants: 'Realities' constructed by open or closed communication systems. XVIth General Assembly International Association of Mass Communication Research, Barcelona 1988.
Newsom, D. A.
Measuring Effectiveness In Public Relations. 11th Public Relations World Congress, Melbourne, Australia, 1988.
Newsome, D. A., Alan Scott and Judy Van Slyke Turk
This is PR. Wadsworth: Belmont, Calif., 1989.
Norton, M.
A Guide To Company Giving. London: The Directory of Social Change, 1988.
Norton, M.
Major Companies and their Charitable Giving. London: The Directory of Social Change, 1989.
Pastin, M.
Hard Problems of Management. San Francisco and London: Jossey Bass, 1986.
Pastin, M.
'What to do about ethics', *Chief Executive Magazine,* no. 46, Jul/Aug, 1988.
Porritt, J.
Friends of The Earth Handbook. London: Macdonald Optima, 1987.
Rassam, C.
Secrets of Success, Sidgwick & Jackson, London, 1988.
Solomon, R. C. and Hanson, K.
It's Good Business. New York: Atheneum Publishers, 1985.
Srivastra, S. and Associates
Executive Integrity. San Francisco and London: Jossey Bass, 1988.

216   *Appendices*

Stevens, E.
Business Ethics. New York/Remsay: Paulist Press, 1979.
Velasquez, M. G.
Business Ethics. Englewood Cliffs, NJ: Prentice Hall, 1982.
Wallace, R. G.
Insight Digest, no. 1, Sept, 1984.
Ward, C.
Company Courtesy: Managing public and personal relations. Aldershot: Gower, 1989.
Winkworth, S.
Great Commercial Disasters. London: Macmillan, 1980.

Index